TOLTECS
OF THE
NEW MILLENNIUM

TOLTECS
OF THE NEW
MILLENNIUM

VICTOR SANCHEZ
TRANSLATED FROM SPANISH BY ROBERT NELSON

BEAR & COMPANY
PUBLISHING
SANTA FE, NEW MEXICO

LIBRARY OF CONGRESS CATALOGING-IN-PUBLICATION DATA

Sanchez, Victor, 1961–
   [Toltecas del Nuevo Milenio. English]
   Toltecs of the new millennium / Victor Sanchez :
translated by Robert Nelson.
   p.cm.
   ISBN 1-879181-35-5
   1. Shamanism—Mexico. 2.Toltecs —Religion. 3. Indians of
Mexico—Religion. 4. Sanchez, Victor. 1961– . I. Nelson,
Robert. II. Title.

BL2370.S5S24513 1996   96-13276
299′.792—dc20   Allen County Public Library   CIP

Bear & Company, Inc.
Santa Fe, NM 87504-2860

Cover design: © 1996 by Lightbourne Images
Cover illustration: © 1990 by Bill Binger
Interior design & illustration: Marilyn Hager
Typography: Marilyn Hager

Printed in the United States by BookCrafters
1 3 5 7 9 8 6 4 2

To the Survivors . . .

CONTENTS

ACKNOWLEDGMENTS

I would like to express my recognition to the following beings, whose presence in the world has contributed in a very significant way toward the realization of the present work.

To my teokaris, the jicareros of Santa Maria, for the simplicity and joy with which they carry out the titanic task of maintaining alive their tradition amid these difficult times.

To Tere and Maria del Mar for their support and impetus in the realization of my madness.

To Manolo, René, and Armando for their friendship and courage in the battles we shared.

To my father, the Sun.

To my mother, the Earth.

To my brother, the Deer.

To my grandfather, the Fire.

To the Spirit.

INTRODUCTION

I do not write these lines out of whim; nor am I interested in presenting myself as the chosen heir for transmitting the Tradition to which I am linked. I write them as part of a task and a responsibility that was revealed to me among indigenous peoples of Toltec descent and that came to me directly from the Spirit. Although I will not relate everything I witnessed having to do with the procedures and body of practices of said Tradition, I will speak of things that I would personally have preferred to keep secret. But this task is not a personal matter. It implies assuming my responsibility as a witness and participant in one of the most profound and powerful spiritual traditions of the Mesoamerican indigenous world. The survival of these traditions at the dawn of the new millennium offers answers to the urgent necessities of change, which members of modern society require in the crisis of our time.

As you will be able to appreciate in the following narrative, I was not "elected" due to any particular quality by an indigenous master possessor of unworldly powers. Rather I "infiltrated" into their separate reality and connected myself with their tradition through agents beyond my comprehension but which had something to do both with the enormous generosity of those people and my persistent efforts.

The principal thesis of this book is that the Toltec Tradition is not a dead tradition to which we can refer only through stories and legends. It is a living tradition with living practitioners among the indigenous peoples of Mexico. Its survival coincides historically with the presence of sincere searchers who put aside the ways of fanaticism, fantasy, or ideology, and in some way exert themselves in a struggle similar to that which characterized the ancient Toltecs and which characterizes the survivors. This tradition is not only surviving at the dawn of the new millennium, it is transforming itself into a seed about to germinate, a seed that points to the rebirth of Toltequity, from a spiritual rather than ethnic point of view.

As I explained in my earlier book, *The Teachings of Don Carlos*, the material that was then presented formed only a part of the work that I have carried out for more than fifteen years both among indigenous peoples and in the formation of development groups. What remained pending was the publication of materials that gave testimony to the other areas of realized work.

The present volume corresponds to the second part of my testimony and it relates to the concrete experience in the indigenous world. Soon I will make known the third element of this trilogy in which I expand upon the origin, nature, and method of my work with the human development groups I have formed.

I am speaking of indigenous peoples, yes. But not those described by anthropologists, transformed through their interpretations into a backward expression of humanity, and bearers of a folklore that sooner or later will end up in museums or in ethnological or historical works, where they will continue to tell us of our cultural richness or our "great historical past".

The I ndians of whom I speak, my brothers of the mountains, have very little to do with what is taught in courses on shamanism, nor are they interested in taking us on as apprentices. They are in their own element, which is quite removed from our artificial world of concepts and concrete. Distance notwithstanding, however, today it is vitally important for us to learn even a little of that in which they are experts: the Encounter with the Spirit and the intimate and harmonic relationship with the Sun, the Earth, and the Fire.

The Indians to whom I refer speak very little and when

they do, they don't sound like a university professor or a Buddhist master. Nor do they walk on walls or cross canyons by levitating. But they have an enormous advantage over the Indian sages of movies and books: They are of flesh and blood. They exist, and anyone who makes sufficient effort can see them.

These indigenous peoples are bearers of their own very efficient Tradition, which does not operate as a body of beliefs or empty religious practices, but rather as an ensemble of precise procedures allowing a person to experience a wide range of perception, much wider than that normally allowed by the culture of modern Western society.

In this work I speak of the way the indigenous survivors of ancient Toltequity look for and encounter the Spirit and the way they relate themselves with the principal powers of Nature. A way in which there are no books, ideas, beliefs, explanations, interpretations, or intermediaries. A way in which the affair is entirely between the individual and "what's out there." No one promises or sells you anything. No one tells you what you will encounter.

I am speaking of an arduous path that lasts an entire lifetime. A difficult path, yes, but real, profound, and tangible. That is the way of the Toltec. No history, no beliefs. Doing and seeing for oneself. Without intermediaries.

The book consists of nine chapters and the epilogues divided in three parts: The first is a general description of the historic presence of the Toltecs; the second deals with the way I got in touch with the Indians descendant from the ancient Toltecs and the main features of their spiritual tradition; the third and most important part of the book is a testimony to some of my experiences living and learning among these extraordinary people, from my first contact with them to the moment I got involved with my whole being in the practice and living of Toltequity.

It should be made clear that I refer to those Indians with

whom I have lived and learned, calling them "Toltecs" as the word was used among the native peoples of Mexico in the sixteenth century. Toltec refers to the Man of Knowledge, the person who has mastered the deepest arts and learning. They, however, do not call themselves Toltecs, but rather Wirrarika.

Another reason for calling them "Surviving Toltecs of Ancient Times" is that they are the direct inheritors of the spiritual culture of the historical Toltecs, beginning with the fusion between the Toltecs and Wirrarika, which occurred after the disintegration of Tula, in the region known as Aztlán.

The Toltecs of the New Millennium are those indigenous peoples of the sierra who against wind and tide have been able to resist the most brutal pressure that for five centuries has been trying to destroy them. They are those who, in the ineffable force of their Tradition, have encountered sufficient resources to give them a foothold in the third millennium without having lost their own paths of search and encounter with the energy that sustains the universe.

But the Toltecs of the New Millennium refers not only to the survivors of ancient Toltequity. They are also those human beings who, amid modern society with all its noise and confusion, are opening pathways to recover the magical heritage that was robbed from us; pathways that bring us to comprehend and revitalize our intimate connection with the Spirit. These new men and women, who—just like our old grandfathers from Tula—uniting themselves with the Sun in the task of illuminating the darkness and the mystery, are the seed of the New Toltequity.

Even when this knowledge awakens sincere interest in those who search for substantial alternatives, it is very important to avoid an invasion of spiritual seekers (and any other kind of invasion) into indigenous territories. It is of vital importance to preserve these zones of refuge, in which the indigenous peoples of Toltec descent have managed to survive, utilizing their geographical isolation as protection

against the presence of whites or mestizos threatening the survival of their material and spiritual culture. For this reason, I
have changed the names of the communities in which I work
and of the people who figure in the story. The truth is that
generally I am not a friend of hiding things or disguising the
facts. But the indigenous peoples themselves have asked me
to avoid as much as possible waking the curiosity of people
that could result in the undesired presence of mestizos or
whites in those areas they with so much difficulty have managed to keep isolated.

The foregoing notwithstanding, I wish to emphasize that
the indigenous peoples of whom I speak are alive and continue with their practices in this very moment. I did not make up
the facts nor did I complement them with fiction as so often
occurs in unconfirmed tales having to do with "indigenous
knowledge," nurtured in many cases more by Western fantasies about the "Indian sage" than by the presentation of concrete experience.

My proposal is that we develop our own paths to encounter the Toltec that lies hidden and waiting inside each one
of us. The principal features of the Way of the Toltec, which
we can follow without invading indigenous communities, are
contained in the work, *The Art of Living Purposefully*.[1] There I
detail the methodology and form of work that I have developed through courses, fieldwork, and workshops that together constitute a proposal of Human Development, nurtured by
indigenous knowledge and the nonconventional encounter
with nature.

What I have learned among the surviving Toltecs is but a
small part of their knowledge. But to experience their everyday
sense of integration with the natural world, and to share their
trips through the unusual possibilities of perception, has made
me face what I consider a fundamental lesson that concerns all

---

[1] In preparation

of us as humans: We are luminous beings. Giving no importance to what our ego and our ideas tell us about ourselves, the essential truth about our nature remains in agreement with what our grandfathers expressed in ancient Tula:

We are children of the Sun!

Our nature is to shine!

Victor Sanchez
Valle de Anahuac, September 1995

Translator's Note

Translating from Spanish presents certain problems—apart from the problems normally encountered when moving from one linguistic universe to another—that relate to the use of gender. In Spanish, the word "su" is used to indicate "his" or "her," depending on the context; on other occasions, the Spanish language uses masculine grammatical forms to indicate either female or male. Changing the gender from the way it appears in the original Spanish text to a more genderless form is, therefore, not always easy, and, on occasions, this style may even change the meaning of a given passage.

The problem is further compounded when the text relates to things spoken originally in an indigenous tongue, or spoken in Spanish by indigenous people. Spanish spoken this way is quite different from "official" Spanish. This difference in the way indigenous people speak Spanish also reflects their view of the world as distinct from that of city dwellers. Ideally, my work as a translator should be to translate into modern English, which, at present, is experiencing a strong movement toward demasculization. However, since this book deals with a society different from ours, with a distinct copy of reality, both the author and I regard the context of the situations as they occurred as being of primary importance, and therefore consider current trends in the English language as secondary.

In situations that refer to the sun, the earth, the water, or the wind, for example, this perspective can readily be appreciated. For native peoples, these are not simply objects existing in the world to be referred to using "it," but rather as "him" or "her" (the Sun and his power, Earth and her lessons of love, the Wind and his unpredictable behavior, the Water and her ability to give life). We find another example in the word "marakame" (the Wirrarika shaman). Although there exist a few women marakames, among the Wirrarika they are so rare that the marakame is always referred to in the masculine form. So, if I were to change this to reflect current English language trends, it would result in a different view of reality than that portrayed by the author's original text. This is why we have decided to leave the text as it appears originally in the Spanish, changing to "he or she," for example, only in those places where the content of the original would remain unaffected. This is solely our decision and does not necessarily reflect the point of view of our English-language publisher.

R.N.

TOLTECS
OF THE NEW
MILLENNIUM

PART
ONE

THE
TOLTEC
TRADITION

ONE

THE HISTORIC TOLTECS

Historical knowledge of the Toltecs, like everything else having to do with our pre-Hispanic past, is scarce and confusing. This is due not only to the lack of written documents or the insufficiency of archaeological findings, but also to the difficulties arising from trying to comprehend civilizations that have a very different perception of the world in relation to the conceptual references of contemporary thought and cosmovision.

How did the Toltecs live? What were they interested in? What kind of world did they perceive? The answers to such questions would be equally difficult if the Toltecs themselves were present here in front of our eyes in this instant. In the same way direct observation of the behavior or way of life of living indigenous peoples does not necessarily give us substantial answers to similar questions. Actually, in spite of the years and years of field observations, studies beginning from the reports of Sahagún[1] to modern anthropological studies, the indigenous universe remains unpenetrated by religious or scientific investigators. This arises from the Eurocentric notion, which in general the rest of the world shares, that there is no universe or reality other than that which we perceive normally. Therefore, the indigenous world, past or present, seen through nonindigenous eyes and thought, is always a distortion from what that indigenous world is in itself, as it is perceived by those who live within it.

All historical studies, ethnological work, and human sciences in general would have to be revised and reestablished beginning with the phenomenalistic donjuanist proposal that the world, such as we perceive it, is a description we received at the time we were born and then learned to construct as we incorporated ourselves into the social world. Thus, if we place an indigenous mazateco and a man from the city in the same room or in the same spot on a mountain, they will find themselves in separate realities and they will see different worlds. While the indigenous man sees in the table of statistics on the wall only lines without meaning, the man of the city looks with worry at the decline in the productivity of his business. While in the woods, the indigenous man listens and learns from the trees, but the business man will only see raw material to be used for commercial purposes. Naturally if the indigenous man were to speak of the lessons he receives from his brothers the trees or of the spirits of the mountain, the city man would think, "Ah, these little superstitious Indians, poor things!" without suspecting that he himself is a prisoner, trapped within his singular vision of the world. Only the Man of Knowledge is capable of crossing the Parallel Lines, which keep the worlds apart, to discover there are countless more worlds to be perceived and experienced. Later I will go into more depth with this theme.

---

[1] See *Historia General de las Cosas de la Nueva España*, Fray Bernardino Sahagun, Editorial Porrua, Mexico, 1984.

Indigenous reality is then extremely elusive and even more so when we are dealing with past reality. The Aztecs themselves, about whom there exist a great number of ethnographic traces and documents written during the time of the arrival of the Spaniards, are a source of debate and controversy, with many different historical views currently coexisting and competing among themselves. The ancient Toltecs, much further back in time, are an enormous mystery about which there exist only legends. Legends the Aztecs told. Legends told by ethnohistorians. Legends told by storytellers in many indigenous communities in Mexico. Legends told by the marakames. Legends told by Men of Knowledge. Legends told by the surviving Toltecs, alive in our time.

On the other hand, and still more important than the legends and stories, is the living testimony: the Toltecs of today who constitute one of the central themes of this book.

I am aware of the almost insurmountable difficulty in wanting to comprehend the indigenous universe from our contemporary Western universe and of the scarcity of information available. Nevertheless, I will comment on some characteristics of the Toltec world that are plainly evident in the legends and indigenous tales, as well as in academic investigations on the subject.

Although official history places the Toltecs in a period stretching from the ninth century to the twelfth, the origins of Toltequity are lost in the darkness of time. Its oldest vestiges can be traced in a line that projected through time could be perceived as the Olmecs-Teotihuacans-Toltecs, and later, after the disintegration of Tula, dividing itself into such varied spheres as the Wirrarikas, Aztecs, and Maya.

QUETZALCOATL

The figure that stands out the most in the Toltec world is without doubt Quetzalcoatl, the Feathered Serpent also called Huemac. Due to his representation in codices and archaeological findings, it is possible to know the Toltec character of many pre-Colombian peoples. He can be observed in the pyramids of Tula, Hidalgo, where can also be found the so-called "Atlanteans." We find him in Xochicalco, Morelos, a meeting place for wise men of many different indigenous groups (they came specifically to deepen Toltec Knowledge, in particular, the multiple aspects of the human-universe relationship). In Chichenitza, Yucatan, the same Plumed Serpent descending the principal pyramid indicates the beginning of spring each March 21 in an amazing effect of shadow, which gives us a minimal example of the profoundness and precision of Maya-Toltec knowledge about the universe. This also occurs in Xochicalco, where a ceremonial grotto is illuminated, through an orifice opening to the outside, precisely on the solstice, signaling the beginning of summer on June 21. The bird-serpent conjunction we find again in the emblem of Meshico Tenochtitlan, which is preserved to date on the flag of Mexico. The examples could go on to cover the greater part of our territory and the Central American countries.

Quetzalcoatl represents many things relating to historical events as well as to symbols of a philosophical and spiritual nature. He is known as the cultural hero and civilizer who carried the Toltecs to their highest level of technical and spiritual development. And although everything seems to indicate that there existed a human Quetzalcoatl who was governor of Tula, the symbol of the Plumed Serpent, representing the elevation of that which before was lowly, transcends the historic personage. He was called Quetzalcoatl precisely for having achieved within his person such spiritual elevation. It should be remembered that in the highest pre-Columbian cultures, religion and science were not separate; rather they formed part of an integral knowledge that allowed an appropriate relationship of the individual with his or her world. Therefore, it is not strange that the knowledge of Quetzalcoatl expresses itself the same in technical-scientific knowledge as in that relative to the development of awareness and a spiritual life.

THE TOLTECS DISPERSE

The mysterious departure or disappearance of Quetzal-coatl is associated with the end of Toltec splendor and there exist many tales and legends dealing with this matter. However it was, toward the end of the twelfth century, Tula was abandoned and the Toltecs disbanded. Wandering, they distributed themselves in different regions of Mesoamerica which, in greater or lesser measure, became enriched by the presence of the Toltec sages. Starting from this period, due to Toltec influence, the Maya attained heights never before reached.

Some of the groups originating from ancient Tula settled in the proximity of Nayarit and Sinaloa five centuries before the Spanish invasion would oblige them to take refuge in the high mountains where to date they can be found. Precisely in that region, from a basically Toltec population was formed the famous Aztlán. From there proceeded the twelve tribes who, after a Pilgrimage of two hundred years following a message from the world of dreaming, founded Meshico Tenochtitlan, giving origin to the Meshica people also known as the Aztecs.[2]

---

[2] See *Historia del Nombre y Fundacion de la Ciudad de Mexico*, Gutierre Tibón, Mexico, 1975.

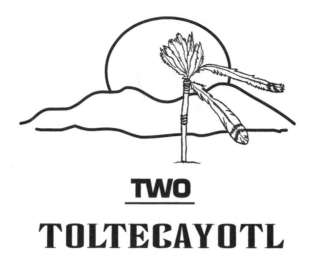

TWO

TOLTECAYOTL

The Toltecs were not a warrior people in the classic sense of the word, meaning they were not dedicated to wars of conquest or similar matters. The Toltecs were a people who held the arts and knowledge in high esteem. Among them the culture of "flower and song"[1] reached its highest expression. They were warriors of the Spirit. The Meshicas[2] themselves called the arts and sciences "Toltecayotl" (Toltequity), and the person of knowledge was "Toltec," the sage.[3]

As they were not focused on warlike activities, the Toltecs centered their interest on Knowledge and the Spirit. The daily life of both simple and principal members of society was devoted fundamentally to religion, which preserved its original character as the Way to the Spirit.

At this point, it would be well to note that for the ancient Toltecs, as well as for those surviving today, religion was not

---

[1] See *La Filosofia Nahuatl*, Miguel León Portilla, UNAM, Mexico, 1990.

[2] Aztecs

[3] See *Toltecayotl*, Miguel León Portilla, F.C.E., Mexico, 1989.

like our modern religions, a standard of predetermined conduct, dogmas, or the projection of human self-importance to
the spheres of the divine, often used manipulate the masses
for the benefit of a small dominant group. Rather it was—as
mentioned—a series of forms and practices whose objective
was to keep people in contact with the Spirit.

From our own perspective, and from our modern concep-
tion of religion, we attempt to observe and comprehend non-
Western religions and we fail. As we interpret pre-Hispanic
religions for example, we fall into the error of believing that
our conceptions having to do with religion are universal.
Thus, if we observe a Wirrarika speaking respectfully of the
Sun, or performing some ritual to link with the energy of the
Earth, we are compelled to think that the Wirrarikas consider
the Earth and the Sun to be their gods. In the face of these
multiple symbols and representations of the abstract, we usually say simply that they "believe in many gods."

The majority of religions made the representations of the
Spirit more and more complicated, to the point where they
took these representations for reality and ended up inventing
God. The ego and self-importance participated actively in the
process and God wound up being in image and likeness to the
human ego, with desires, anger, the need for recognition and
praise, and so forth. At this point, religion came to "believe"
in all these tales invented collectively about "God" and to act
in accordance with codes of conduct derived from such tales,
which "casually" just happened to coincide with the private
interests of the group in power.

It did not happen like that among the ancient Toltecs, nor
does it happen that way among some surviving ethnic groups
of Toltequity, who keep their original religion almost intact
and therefore continue to be a true way to the encounter with
the Spirit.

Another relevant aspect of Toltec spirituality expressed in
their religion is its pragmatism, as we can observe in this short
talk I had with don Pedro de Haro, one of the most powerful

and respected marakames of the Wirrarikas in the sierras, during my stay in San Sebastian.

"No son, you people think that we Indians are fools, no? Because we believe in many gods and who knows how many other things. But our religion, unlike that of the tewaris (mestizos or whites) is not a matter of believing but rather of seeing. Look, I'll tell you what I told a gringo, one of those who call themselves pastors[4] and who believe that we are all his flock. He was obstinate, and letting on about Christ here, and the Bible there, and then I told him: 'Now, now, let's see? How do you know if Christ did or if Christ didn't? Well? Did you know him?'

'Well, not in person.'

'And have you known anyone who knew him in person?'

'Of course not, he lived two thousand years ago.'

'Two thousand years??? You're kidding! And how do you know if he existed or if they're nothing but fables?'

'Well, we have his word here in the Bible.'

'Oh, man we are lost! I don't even know how to read! And then you tell us that Indians are stupid because we believe in the Earth and the Sun!

'Stupid, stupid! But nobody tells me about Tatei Urianaka (the Earth), I see her every day! And every day I receive her fruits, corn, water, and beans. I can touch, walk, and live on her! And Tau (the Sun). Daily I receive his heat and his *nierika* (light, knowledge, vision, teaching). I don't have to do anything but look up and there he is.

'And besides what did Christ produce? As far as I know he never produced anything, while the Earth, on the other hand, just look at her. All the time she is producing! And she feeds us and that's how we live. So? Who are the fools?'

"Well, we got rid of him, that's why none of those kind have ever been able to enter here, not them nor the others[5]!"

---

[4] preacher

[5] "Others" refers to the Catholic priests.

THE SPIRIT

The intuition of the Great Spirit is inherent in humans. The feeling of being incomplete or alone has accompanied us throughout all of our history. And it is not due merely from fear or weakness that we have invented gods. The fact is that behind or at the bottom of all that exists lies an ultimate energy that animates and moves everything existing. The ancient Chinese called it the Tao, modern physicists simply call it energy, the Maya Hunab-ku, the Wirrarika Tatewari or Iusi, the ancient Toltecs Ometeotl or the Eagle, and the warriors of the new Toltequity call this all-sustaining force Mystery, Nagual, Intent, or simply Spirit. However, names are the least important since what really counts is the link that, by our acts, we are able to maintain with that energy.

The objective of the person who goes to Knowledge is— from the Toltec perspective—to encounter the Spirit and be one with it, expressing its natural flow through everyday actions. Flowing and behaving in accordance with the Spirit, our actions do not encounter insurmountable obstacles; rather they are efficient, harmonious, and powerful, besides giving us peace and well-being. Thus, all of our difficulties arise from the fact and from the moment in which the individual, or society as a whole, loses awareness of its link with the Spirit and therefore acts in discord with the natural flow of energy.

NATURE: THE VISIBLE FACE OF THE SPIRIT

Every part of the existing world is nothing other than the visible face of the Spirit, but people—blinded by their own feelings of importance—have lost the awareness of their relation with the Spirit and therefore feel themselves to be separate from everything, aspiring even to be above everything. Nature, on the other hand, is not a victim of the spell of reason and therefore she expresses in a natural way the flow of the Spirit. This is why many Men of Knowledge have had as "teachers" a ravine, a mountain, or a tree, while others have become apprentices of a wolf or a deer, to list some examples.

Toltec Knowledge, not having devolved into religious forms empty of the Spirit, has as one of its fundamental aspects the observation and relation of humans with nature. It does not place us as the king of creation, nor as the highest and most developed element in nature, rather to the contrary; aware of our dangerous tendency to remain spellbound by our own thoughts, it realizes that we are the ones who need to learn from nature, in order to reintegrate ourselves and occupy the place that naturally belongs to us within her. This difference between our religious concepts and those of the world of Toltequity remains manifest in the fact that, while for us in Western culture, God is bearded (male, naturally) and often wrathful, the Wirrarika represent the energy that governs the world as a blue deer.

Today, modern people, tied to our compulsive anthropocentrism, consider the "worship of nature" a primitive form of religion that preceded the modern concept in which one god, with human form and characteristics, is worshipped. However, this is nothing more than another form of the arrogance displayed by Western culture. We insist on putting ourselves at the center of everything, viewing nature and everything in it as inferior, a simple accumulation of resources placed there exclusively for satisfying our needs and desires. This suicidal attitude of continuing to harm the environment in order to satisfy the compulsive need to accumulate more and more capital is but one of the consequences of said arrogance. This should bring us to reconsider our point of view regarding the backward "worship of nature." Isn't it much more reasonable and even urgent that we learn again to feel respect and veneration for the Earth, the Sun, the mountains, the rivers, and the animals?

We damage nature, use and abuse her, because we consider ourselves outside of her. We don't accept that we ourselves are part of her and in destroying her, we are destroying ourselves as well. The spiritual practices of indigenous peoples, so tied to nature, are and were a much more reasonable way to relate to the environment from which they derive a healthy, rather than suicidal, use of natural resources.

This spiritual feeling nourished their technical-scientific activity as well, from which it was not divorced, allowing for large population centers in pre-Hispanic Mexico without a growing deterioration of the environment.

THE WAY OF TOLTEC KNOWLEDGE

Following this same perspective, the initiation of a Toltec to Knowledge is not an exclusively human affair, not determined by the existence of a teacher and a student. The apprentice learns from nature and ultimately from the Spirit. The presence of sorcerers, healers, or marakames is not to transmit knowledge from themselves to an apprentice, but basically to push those wanting to learn so that they establish contact with the Spirit, which indicates true knowledge. This is why Toltec Men of Knowledge rarely speak; their techniques of teaching—besides setting an example—constitute an enormous range of activities and complex procedures, which must be carried out by those who work and learn from them. Such procedures tend to open the door to Silent Knowledge, which is a hidden possibility in every human being.

In the indigenous rituals of initiation, it is not an adult or teacher who initiates the apprentices, but rather they initiate themselves with nature. The young man, to convert himself into a warrior, has to carry out a long hike over unknown mountains and territories, to search for a magic deer who gives lessons in how to live. The ritual to be carried out before sunrise, the cathartic dance or ritual to be performed before the power of a thunderstorm, the learning gained during the arduous ascent of a sacred mountain—these are examples of this teaching realized through a relationship with nature.

I recall a conversation I had with Agustin, a young Wirrarika from Santa Maria.

"And you, Agustin, have you gone to Humun' Kulluaby?"

"Not yet, but maybe soon."

"And why haven't you gone yet?"

"Well, because I'm afraid. It's really scary! One doesn't go for pleasure, but rather out of obligation."

"Why do you say that? What do you go for?"

"Well, to *see*! There is where Tamatzin (Tamatz Kahullumary, the great-grandfather tail of the deer) tells you what you are going to do—if you will dedicate yourself to the land, or to curing, or to singing, or to being a marakame. Just for these things I'm telling you, you need to struggle a lot, and that's why I'm afraid. If you don't do everything well, then you see purely horrible things, devils and things like that."

"And if, for example, you want to be a healer, who teaches you? Another healer?"

"No, of course not. First you receive a sign there in Humun' Kulluaby. If the deer speaks to you and tells you: 'Listen you! You're going to be a healer,' then you have to be a healer."

"And how do you begin? Who teaches you?"

"Nobody, one has to learn by oneself."

"But how! If nobody teaches you, how can you learn to heal?"

"Well, like I told you. Look, if he who has received a sign goes home, but does not begin because he lacks confidence, he makes a fool of himself in good time. Although he has already received the order, if he still is too afraid to begin, then the deer appears in his dreams and tells him: 'What are you waiting for? Begin now!' And so the deer follows him, pestering and pestering him while the would-be healer does nothing. Until one day, one of the members of his family falls ill and he has no choice and he has to heal that person as best he can, with herbs, chanting, by drawing the sickness out with his mouth, anyway he can! And that's how he starts. When another member of his family becomes ill, he also heals him or her. He can do it since Tamatzin gave him this Gift. And so he is now a healer."

"And once he cures those of his family, does he announce to the rest of the Wirrarika that he can cure?"

"No, he says nothing to no one, but his neighbors gradually come to know him as a healer and when someone becomes sick they look for him and so his fame grows, according to how successful he is."

For the same reason it is not merely a human knowledge. The Knowledge of the warriors of Toltequity did not consist, nor does it consist, of words learned in books or heard from the teachers' lips. Although words exist between the apprentice and the person who pushes him or her toward knowledge, these play a secondary role, and are useful generally after the apprentice has personally experienced Knowledge.

For the true experience of Knowledge there are no books, teachings, teachers, or words.

The only Way is the life itself, the only Teacher is the Spirit and its visible face: nature.

TEACHING YOURSELF

In the Náhuatl language[6] there exists no concept of learning as it is conceived in the West, where we learn from someone else, specifically a teacher. In that tongue the word closest to the English phrase "to learn" would be *nimomashtic*, translated literally as teaching yourself. Thus I was told by my first "teachers" of Wirrarika dance—two children who encouraged me during a long ritual: "teach yourself, teach yourself!"

This is why we who truly assume the responsibility that signifies the Way of Knowledge clearly understand that masters, books, or groups are only aids of greater or lesser value according to circumstances. They are to be used for our own battle toward Knowledge and Freedom, at which we will arrive by our own efforts and our own will, taking our own

---

[6] Náhuatl was the language of the Toltecs, Aztecs, and many other indigenous peoples from ancient and contemporaneous Mexico.

steps with our own energy. And in any case, the only indispensable elements needed are a ready Spirit and the necessary energy to begin the Way. If these are present, the external aids will appear, in whatever form. On the other hand, if we lack internal conviction or the necessary energy, all the greatest masters, all the books read, all the courses taken, cannot help us.

In the era in which we live, the "teach-yourself" that our old grandparents knew is especially relevant; the time of the masters has passed and the time has arrived for each one of us to assume our own responsibility. This is not the time to put the only true inheritance we have, that is to say our one and only life, into the hands of masters or guides, whether they be genuine or not. Considering it carefully, if we can deal directly with the Spirit, why do we need intermediaries? Your time has arrived and it's here and now. Use it!

PART
TWO

THEY ARE
STILL HERE

THREE

LOOKING
FOR THE
TOLTECS

THE TOLTEQUITY AMONG
THE MEXICAN INDIANS

I use the word "Toltec" as it was used by the Aztecs at the time of the arrival of the Spaniards, long after the disappearance of the historic Toltecs. Thus they called a Man of Knowledge, and "Toltequity" was the task that, according to stories, legends, and ethnographic and archaeological testimonies, characterized the ancient Toltecs expressing their vocation toward things having to do with Knowledge and the return to the Spirit. From this perspective, we call Toltecs those groups that bear a marked influence from the historical Toltecs or share their active interest for Knowledge and its specific expressed forms, even though they may not so be classified from an ethnohistorical viewpoint.

Toltequity was present in many other indigenous groups

of the pre-Columbian era. We can find Toltec influence in almost all Mesoamerican peoples and in South American cultures.

Although the conquest and later colonization of indigenous territories literally wiped out entire peoples, some survived and with them Toltequity survived as well. The degree to which the surviving groups have preserved their ethnic structure up to the end of the twentieth century has been very diverse, depending on many factors such as geographical location, density of population, and internal cohesion.

Thus, there exist groups who remain relatively pure from a racial point of view, but who have lost their language and original culture. There also exist those who have been able to withstand pressure of all types, keeping their culture, religion, and way of life almost intact. It is among the latter that the footprints of Toltec Knowledge are kept fresh.

Such an achievement has not been easy. For five hundred years the Indians have been at the bottom rung of Mexican national society. First there were the Spanish soldiers and their firearms. After that came the church and colonial administration. Later came the national integrationist projects, actually aimed at the disintegration of Indian nations and native peoples. Capitalists, political bosses, and landowners have stolen their lands and converted them into peons—almost slaves— with miserable salaries. In more recent times—helped by modern technology and strong economic resources—the church, both national and international, has seen in them a new and substantial clientele for their religious proselytism. Whether through physical disappearance, through disappearance of their culture, or fusion into the mestizo society, the portion of the indigenous population that maintains a clear connection with its roots has diminished drastically.

All these factors—the conquest, illnesses brought over from Europe, forced evangelization, the colonial period, capitalist development, and industrialization—have been nibbling inch by inch at the ancient indigenous territory for half a millennium, to the point where the ancient cultures of "flower and song" have almost disappeared. Each one of these outside forces has struggled with all the means at its disposal to force the Indian peoples to renounce their culture, their religion, their way of being, and their pride. Those who arrived from outside, taking possession of everything, have insisted and continue to insist, but the native peoples of Mexico and the Americas will not yield. They remain standing, although in order to do so they have had to leave their original territories on the plains and take refuge in the most inaccessible mountain ranges.[1]

These peoples in breasting the tide have been able to defend their way of being at all costs. They are responsible for the fact that today, just at the beginning of the new millennium, Toltequity with its practices and rituals remains alive.

In Mexico there currently exist fifty-seven ethnic groups, besides the mestizo population. Among the most numerous of these we could name the Náhuas, Mazatecos, Wirrarika, Zapatecos, Otomies, Totonacas, Yaquis, and Tarahumaras. Each ethnic group has defended in its own way its own identity. Some seem to be acculturated[2] since they have adopted the mestizo way of dressing and they speak Spanish. Nevertheless, careful observation often reveals the persistence of an internal, basically indigenous, way of being in spite of their external appearance.

One of the most lamentable aspects in this process of the loss of ethnic identity is what is called the "stigma" of the indigenous condition. Due to the miserable conditions in which the majority of indigenous peoples find themselves, many of them feel ashamed of being Indians. Seeing the white or the mestizo as someone who supposedly has money, health, and well-being, they try to "mestizise" themselves,

---

[1] See *Regiones de Refugio*, Gonzalo Aguirre Beltrán, Instituto Indigenista Interamericano, Mexico City, 1967.

[2] to have lost their original culture

rejecting their own language, their traditional form of dress and so forth. It is common in many communities to hear the elders complain about the lack of interest of the young in the customs of their ancestors. With all this, they survive in a world where poverty and hunger are extreme. They cannot be judged.

Fortunately, not all indigenous peoples have been as unfortunate. There are those who keep their language, dress, religion, and customs virtually without contamination. They are scarcer and more difficult to contact, but their significance for our current era is of great importance, since they are the true carriers of the sacred traditions of pre-Hispanic Mexico.

THE TOLTEC CONNECTION

I have had the chance to travel over large areas in my country of Mexico, concerning myself especially with those regions where nature reigns almost without interference from people. It seems incredible, but fortunately places like that still exist in our country. In my search for an encounter with nature and her equilibrium, I found myself with those who for centuries have known how to live in harmony with her—the Indians of Mexico. I have known and lived with different groups and indigenous communities—Náhuas, Tzotziles, Tzeltales, Mazatecos, Matlatzincas, Wirrarika, Mixtecos, Zapotecos and Totonacas. Among them, I have savored my most definitive experiences with the Náhuas and Wirrarika, giving me the strong impression that these two groups have most purely preserved ancient Toltec knowledge. The Náhuas are direct descendants of the population of Tula, and the Wirrarika are geographically near to the Toltecs of Aztlán. But beyond geographical, migratory, or genealogical associations lies the persistent spiritual attitude with which these groups harmonize themselves with the Toltecs of antiquity.

I have been able to make contact with spiritual traditions, methods of Knowledge and expansion of awareness that have been preserved in diverse forms among indigenous peoples. To make them more comprehensible, we can classify them into three categories.

The first and most general is the cosmovision, of pre-Hispanic origin, which practically all the members of the indigenous community share. Such Knowledge can be found (if we have the capacity to see beyond our own culture) in almost any individual of the community in question. It includes the awareness of death, the intimate relationship with nature, the awareness of the Earth as a living being, the awareness of the dreaming body (among the Wirrarika).

The second category refers to knowledge, methods, practices, and rituals performed by individuals or special groups within the community. Among the Wirrarika for example, any marakame, or the principal marakame of the community and the group of "jicareros"[3] he directs, is recognized by the entire community as being in charge of everything relating to the religious activities of the community. But at the same time, there is maintained an entire series of practices unknown to those who do not form part of this select group of initiates.

In the third category are found the *lineages*—small groups of individuals who, generation after generation through oral tradition have preserved specific practices of ancient knowledge, in complete secrecy, and in such a way that the existence of these lineages passes unnoticed even by the rest of the com-

---

[3] The jicareros are a spiritual group whose members are charged with the keeping of the Tradition. There are about thirty of them and each one represents one of the original spirits who gave origin to the world and to the Tradition itself. Consequently their lives in general and their specific tasks maintain a precise relation to those actions that, in agreement with the story of the creation of the world—according to the Wirrarika—were carried out by each one of the original spirits or "kakayares." They are directed by a marakame—also known as "singer"—who, in holding this reponsibility, is considered the principal marakame of the community.

munity of which they form a part. Its members appear to others as peasants, merchants, artisans, healers, or however they choose to appear. In very recent times, and in a highly exceptional manner, these lineages have included nonindigenous individuals in their practices.

Although I have made contact with this Tradition under the three forms mentioned, for now I can only recount publicly my experiences relating to the first two categories, only very indirectly referring to the third.

NÁHUAS AND WIRRARIKA:
THE SURVIVING TOLTEQUITY

It was among the Náhuas that I experienced my birth as a warrior of Toltequity, which more than a membership or title, represents a disposition toward life, in which we struggle to make each act a challenge and each task undertaken one more step toward the Spirit. This took place in a Náhuatl community, surrounded by high mountains in Central Mexico. Said community was peculiar in that it preserved intact the ancient rites of linking with the awareness of the Earth, which provoked in those participating a very special perceptive awareness—unknown to most people—that Carlos Castaneda calls the second attention.[4] This was in spite of the fact that in the town there exists a very large and ancient church that dates from the sixteenth century.

The presence of a Catholic priest has been part of community life for centuries. And for centuries each priest in turn has struggled to eradicate what are considered pagan, even satanic, practices of the Indians. The first time I came to this community, they—the new priest as well as the indigenous members each in their own way—told me that the previous

---

[4] "The second attention represents an unknown and very specialized use of the attention. It permits us to perceive another, practically limitless, part of reality that could well be called another world since it is so foreign to our world of everyday affairs." From *The Teachings of Don Carlos*, Victor Sanchez, Bear & Company, Santa Fe, 1995.

priest had left the community less than a year before. He was a very old and somewhat irritable man who had struggled for ten years, with all the means at his disposal, to eradicate the persistent "idolatry" of the place. This male saint was highly offended that the Indians of the community—all year pretending to act like "good Christians"—would, without warning, suddenly disappear from their houses and little huts to spend three days participating in rites of pre-Hispanic origin having to do with the worship of the Earth. This happened in some secret caves relatively nearby, which the angry priest could not find no matter how hard he tried. This occurred year after year, and since the date was variable—tied to the unfolding of the agricultural cycle more than to the calendar—there was no way the priest could know when it would occur. He did everything he could, even organizing pilgrimages with a triumphant Christ figure to "exorcise" the various surrounding mountains. To no avail. These little Indians were extremely stubborn. On Sundays at mass, especially after they had mysteriously disappeared for three days, the priest would angrily scold them and he did it in Náhuatl since he had learned to speak it fluently. Thus in their own tongue he reprimanded them in church, calling them devil worshipers. He used a Náhuatl word the Indians never pronounce, since among them, as among other peoples of Toltec descent, the word has a meaning that summons magic. To name something is to summon it, attract it.

Well, it happened that this man threatened them with damnation, naming the devil time and time again. The natives (the few that attended mass) did not know where to hide when this man dared to "summon the devil in the house of God!" They became very nervous and had no desire to return to the church. One fine day there occurred the most logical thing under such circumstances. It was a typical rainy day in the mountains, in which it doesn't merely rain, it pours, and a storm let loose with much lightning and thunder. Suddenly a lightning bolt penetrated the church, precisely striking the altar and burning it completely. The priest was so scared that he fled. For the natives it was completely natural—a small price to pay for the enormous offense of summoning the devil in the house of God. I never met the famous priest, but I could see the effects of the lightning on the burned altar. The last time I was there, in the early nineties, these rituals of remembering the Earth were alive and well and the caves in question still remained secret.

In this place I had the good fortune to be accepted as an "adopted son" by one of those in charge of organizing and protecting the practice of the rituals and the caves as well as the great stone figures of pre-Colombian origin found within. As far as I know, I thus became the only person ever, outside the indigenous community, to learn the location of the caves and the nature of the rituals practiced there. Of course, I have never revealed their precise location.

"CASTANEDIAN" PRACTICES

If my birth as a warrior in the Toltec lineage occurred among the Náhuas, my "coming of age" was attained among the Wirrarika. They, as an ethnic group, seem to me to be the most "Toltec" of those I have known, due to the nature of their practices and rituals, as well as to their way of everyday life. I encountered among them the concrete experience of much of what had been dreams, things that intellectually seemed attractive to me without knowing truly whether they existed or not. At the time of my first contact with the Wirrarika, I had already covered some distance with what I had experienced among the Náhuas as well as the search for true growth in my daily life that begins always with our own internal being. One of the efforts I was making along this line derived from reading the books of Carlos Castaneda—his themes and the Knowledge to which they allude were very similar to those I had found myself among the indigenous peoples in the mountains. As the practices derived from these readings were one of the factors that endowed me with the tools enabling me to assimilate my experiences among the Wirrarika, I consider it appropriate here to make a brief digression to discuss them.

Practices such as the observation of not-doing, orienting oneself in darkness using corporal perception, the gait of power, the awareness of death, the second attention, exercises of a nonordinary relationship with the awareness of the Earth, stopping the internal dialogue, connecting with the awareness of trees, and the pragmatic utilization of dreams, among many others, were relatively familiar to me due to my experience among the Náhuas. Nevertheless, a large part of what Castaneda wrote was for me only tales of power. Even though his works occupied an important place in my life, they did not impel me to search for don Juan or for Carlos.

The silent observation of nature and the Knowledge without words of the surviving Toltecs had made it quite clear how not to become entangled in the fantasy of the master as the way to freedom or Knowledge. Castaneda himself was very clear on this point. In place of searching for a nagual, I proceeded with my own energy following the premise of don Juan Matus: "A warrior is impeccable when he trusts his personal power, whether it be small or enormous."[5] Alone, I began to practice the extravagant donjuanesque techniques, which came to be added to what I already knew. I made long and repeated walks of attention, I buried myself, I spent nights suspended in a tree, I did recapitulation, not-doings of the personal self, energy inventories. I looked for ways to erase my personal history, until I came to *see*. Many and prolonged were my experiences in what I called "the living study of the works of Carlos Castaneda." The results were earthshaking: the techniques worked and they revealed an unusual

[5] See *Journey to Ixtlan*, Carlos Castaneda, Penguin Books Ltd, Harmondsworth, Middlesex, England, 1974.

form of awareness, the awareness of the other self, which implied innumerable hidden resources inside every one of us. They revealed forms of perception and utilization of our energy in terms very distinct from the ordinary[6].

Besides the "rare phenomena" that so often capture the attention of readers (allies, talking or listening to trees or the Earth, the sensation of flying, perceiving like a wolf, running in the dark, awareness of the dreaming body, etc.), the Castanedian practices offered me something that is ultimately far more important. I found that don Juan was right: The world we perceive, such as the self (our own ego), is nothing more than a description—a fantasy that only seems real due to our insistence in acting as though it were real. Stopping the world, stopping the self, is much more than extraordinary visual effects. It is nothing more and nothing less than the realized possibility of experiencing worlds, ways of being, and perception differently. Differently and better. If we stop our contradictory description of the world, which we con-struct daily, we see that it is the true path to freedom that allows us to construct better worlds for us to inhabit. Stopping the description of ourselves based on self-importance, com-plaints, frustrations, and meanness is the concrete way to the freedom to choose how to be, according to the different situa-tions in which we find ourselves. We cease to be a slave to only one way of being. We finish with the slavery determined by our personal history. We break the narrow artificially creat-ed limits that determine our self image. We say good-bye to being and living unilaterally.

The practice of the Castanedian techniques allowed me to discover, in short, that we are free. We can *choose* how to be and how to live.

I had been experimenting with Castaneda's techniques for only a short time when I had my first experience with the Wirrarika. At the beginning, like most urban observers, I

---

[6] I have detailed the way in which I applied the Castanedian proposals in *The Teachings of Don Carlos: Practical Applications of the Works of Carlos Castaneda*, Bear & Company, Santa Fe, 1995.

could only look—from the outside—at what they did. I did not realize that, beyond what my eyes and my mind could register, those people were interacting in a separate reality that I could not even imagine. (In the following chapters I will refer to that period of time.)

The passage of time and the events of my life allowed me to gather the necessary energy to take the definitive step and "jump" into the separate reality. That crossing of parallel lines finally revealed to me what I had at once both feared and desired—those tales of power could be transformed into reality. It was not the same to play intellectually with concepts like "non-ordinary reality," which I supposedly took very seriously, as it was to confirm bodily that this separate reality existed and could be shared with other human beings for days or entire weeks. It is easily said, but it requires much effort and an unbending purpose to induce us to act in spite of fear or sadness, which come to us when we find ourselves in worlds and realities for which we are not prepared. The true difficulty in penetrating into parallel worlds is that we are unable to accept them. How can we accept them when our ego's security rests entirely on the continuity we attribute to our everyday world, no matter how absurd and ephemeral it may be? How can we accept the unknown when for all our lives we have learned to fear and to deny all that is not known to us?

The negation of the unknown is an intrinsic characteristic of Western culture that has taken hold of much of the planet, but it is not this way with all peoples on Earth. Among indigenous peoples for example, the existence of unexplainable multiple phenomena is a normal occurrence in their everyday lives. They are accustomed to living with the Mysterious. They assume without difficulty that there are things that can be explained and others that cannot. Since self-importance does not occupy the center of their culture, the unknown does not offend them. This allows them to experience both the explainable reality (*tonal*) and the unexplainable (*nagual*).

The opposite occurs with modern people. Our security and sense of self-importance come from feeling that we know everything, that we can explain everything. For this reason if something new presents itself to our observation, we quickly convert it into the known; we make all kinds of mental associations to transform the unknown and be able to say: "Yes, I already know this! It looks like such and such a thing which I studied, knew, or saw on some such occasion." In an extreme case, if what appears before us does not fit within what we already know, we simply will not see it, even though it is in front of our eyes. We won't even be aware of what is happening to us!

Without a doubt the price we pay for our self-importance is very high—to stay trapped within a single world (and quite a limited one at that) when we could inhabit so many varied and far richer worlds during the time we are alive! The possibility of attaining such worlds is accomplished fundamentally with the extra energy we will have available if we achieve the lessening of our self-importance and reincorporate the mysterious into our lives. Ultimately everything is a question of having sufficient *personal power*.

Returning to the Wirrarika, we could say—in general—that they inhabit a reality separate from the one we normally know. The majority of them are found in what we could call "the periphery of the separate reality." Others—who are most dedicated to the Spirit and who have a high level of energy—inhabit much deeper regions of said reality. Living among them produced in me a "pull" toward their separate reality and made me experience things far more extraordinary than my most fantastic illusions.

THE TOLTECS OF THE MOUNTAINS

My Wirrarika friends are basically human beings occupied with their affairs. I "infiltrated" into their world thanks to their generosity and my persistence. They did not need me for what they were doing and probably I even disturbed them a little. The Knowledge (astounding) in which they are immersed is absolutely nonverbal; rather it consists of practices and concrete experiences. There are no explanations or instructions. They learn by doing, not thinking. Its preservation does not imply sacred books, priests, or religious hierarchy, nor even an oral tradition, since the main part is preserved through a body of practices sustained from generation to generation.

The indigenous peoples of which I speak in this book do not share the same scale of values that seems normal for us in modern society. They are in another world that cannot be imagined without direct experience. What makes them admirable is not the action of prodigies defying the laws of physics (of which we know so little) or the execution of paranormal phenomena, nor the possession of supernatural powers. What makes them admirable is that they love and respect the world of nature, not personal importance and its projections like we do. They know and utilize pragmatically the *nagualic* aspect of human awareness and of the world, while we know little or nothing about it. They are admirable because they are different. Their difference makes them masters of a magical knowledge right before our eyes, although they have no interest in teaching us anything, since they are too busy learning. Their difference allows them to experience extraordinary facets of reality and perception very difficult to describe to anyone who has not lived it with them. This does not mean looking for the unusual for its own sake; rather it implies major results having to do with leading a full and balanced, as well as intense, life. Life is richer when it embodies the unknown face of reality and of ourselves; and on this subject my indigenous friends, the survivors of ancient times, know a great deal. And they are admirable above all because they are alive and exist right now in this world. To achieve that, they have had to survive for more than five centuries against an unending struggle to annihilate them, against Western society, which remains obsessed with destroying all that is different, all that does not reflect or confirm it.

One of the things that caught my attention among the Toltec survivors is that in their spiritual practices, as in their lives, there are no *representations of things*. They really live them. When they are engaged in confession it is not done "as if" they were confessing; they really confess. When they are in front of Grandfather Fire they don't do it "as if" they were communicating with him; they open their hearts completely, they speak and they listen. We experienced an example of this one night during a "deer hunt" after the sacred Pilgrimage. My friend Manolo remembers: "That night did not seem special. They danced for a while but soon all went to sleep. I felt very nostalgic since the idea of the city compared to magic we were experiencing did not appeal to me. I could not sleep and I began to take notes by the light of the fire. Later, when it seemed that nothing else would happen and while immersed in my writing (a song), I received the last great gift of the journey. I had been writing a while when the sensation of movement nearby caused me to look up. Everyone was asleep. Antonio (the great marakame) slowly straightened up, approached the fire and began to speak to it, with feeling . . . tremendous, total. To this man, I did not exist, but all his feeling saturated me. It was as though he was speaking with someone very intimate; he paused, and THE FIRE ANSWERED HIM. I don't know how it happened, but it answered him. The communication was evident. Marakame Antonio wept, and then quickly, as suddenly as it began, it ended. He turned around and went back to sleep. Where is this man? What world is he experiencing in these moments? I could clearly feel that what was happening was wonderful. The vision of the world these people have is in the perception of those living beings who accompany them actively: the Grandfather Fire, the Brother Deer, the Father Sun, the Mother Earth. There is no imagination, explanations, complaints, or judgments. Only impeccability. Overcome with emotion, there remained nothing left for me to do but weep."

They don't pretend to "hunt deer" in Humun' Kulluaby.[7] They really live a commitment in which they put all their being, without reservation, into encountering their deer, which is the vision that teaches them "the correct way to live." Compared to them, we of modern society seem like beings who are always lying, doing things as though they were important, *as though* we really love, *as though* we were important, *as though* we were sincere, *as though* we like our work, *as though* we enjoy our vices, *as though* our struggles are really our own—as though, always "as though." This is why I usually say I like these human beings so much because they *are real* in each one of their acts. A little of that ingrained in us, if only we were to learn in a small way how to be like them, would be an enormous gain.

---

[7] One of the most sacred places of the Wirrarika, the goal of their main pilgrimage. They call it "the paradise."

FOUR

THE
TASK

THE DEER OF HUMUN' KULLUABY[1]

I also went to Humun' Kulluaby looking for my deer. And I found him. There remains with me much more from this encounter than just a beautiful memory. There remains with me the commitment to take it upon myself to respond to what the deer told me. My deer has two antlers: one of them, which refers to my struggle to becomes a *real* person and to live a *true* life, has to do with my personal world and is present in everything I do; the other has to do with the world in which I live, with the time and space that I share with the people of this generation and era. This last point was made clear to me at the end of my stay in Humun' Kulluaby during the descent from the Sacred Mountain La' Unarre, also known as "The Palace of the Governor" (the Sun) or simply "The Palace." There, while running behind the marakame and the

---

[1] See footnote 7 in chapter 3.

urukuakame, I was given instructions on what I should write in this book. I could not intellectually establish where this instruction came from, but it was very clear to me it was a *command* I could not disobey. And here I am.

There, the voice also dictated to me the title it would have: *Toltecs of the New Millennium*. This title alludes to the fact that in this precise moment, just at the dawn of the new millennium and for a brief span of time, there coincide in this world two different types of Toltecs: the surviving Toltecs of the ancient era (Wirrarika and other indigenous groups); and the new seed of Toltecs who, in the time after the domination of the Indian peoples, will take in their hands the "Cup of Knowledge," not in founding schools or churches but in the adoption of ways of life congruent with the Spirit.

This new emerging Toltequity has in this moment the opportunity and the responsibility to make use of the presence of the surviving Toltecs of ancient times, not so much through physical contact with them, which is done very rarely, if at all, as through the development of actions that harmonize with the same Toltec Spirit that moves them. These actions begin with each one of us making the decision to take the responsibility for our own growth and reencounter with the Spirit. By doing so, we will be making ourselves brothers and sisters with the indigenous peoples of the mountains, those who are submerged completely in the task. This moment in which we live is special for three reasons: (1) there still are marakames in intimate relation with Grandfather Fire, with our Mother Tatei Urianaka (Tlaltipac, Earth, Gaia, etc.), and with the Spirit itself; (2) the channel of communication is open; and (3) the ways of return are visible, which increases our possibilities of success in the search for contact. It is up to us now to learn to keep these channels open and to use the ways of the Return to the Spirit while they are still here, before we remain only ourselves alone.

Together, the indigenous survivors—direct inheritors of the ancient Toltec Spirit—and the sincere and determined searchers, alone or in groups, who are waging a battle to realize the way of return, make up that special group. They are privileged by the wonder of being awake and burdened with the responsibility of not forgetting. These I have termed "The Toltecs of the New Millennium."

To comply exactly with the task in which I am immersed, I have to be able to carry out much more than what I have done up until now. Writing for example is not something that comes natural to me. In reality I am not a writer, though for brief periods, I behave as though I were. I write when there is clearly no other way. The solitary exercise of writing is very far from what comes most natural to me—to be in the midst of the act of discovery, which often occurs on an external and internal level simultaneously, whether in remote and inaccessible regions of nature or of reality.

BEYOND ANTHROPOLOGY

I am aware that indigenous reality can be examined from many angles, including the habitual ones of anthropology. Nevertheless, my work has dealt above all with those areas in which academics cannot penetrate because of attachment to their academic formation and their condition as "civilized" men or women. Experiencing for ourselves these unsuspected facets of awareness and perception and interacting with unknown aspects of reality has for us a very great meaning and repercussion for our time and everyday way of existing. The experience opens the door for us to an encounter we need to recover the equilibrium we lost many years ago as persons, and many centuries or millennia ago as humanity. This is the reason why my work is not carried out exclusively in the indigenous world; rather there is a counterpart, in all the work I do among the non-indigenous, among the people of the cities involved in the problems of modern life.

Social or ethnological anthropology should be the channel by which we become familiar with the unknown of "the others" (the Indians, for example). In reality it is a small closed universe that both begins within academic boundaries and directs itself toward these same boundaries where it looks for approval. The reality of "the others" is touched upon very superficially, if at all. People on the street are not likely to obtain any benefit, gain, or transformation—they do not even know what anthropologists do. Beneficiaries of anthropological labors are not the indigenous peoples or the people of society or even themselves as individuals. Beneficiaries are their superiors in government offices and other anthropologists who qualify and validate each other's work.

I wished to deal with precisely those areas that academic investigators did not wish to or could not discover, or whose existence they suspected, but did not enter into. If they had searched and found, they would not have dared to state so publicly for fear of losing "scientific precision" or the recognition of their colleagues of the academic establishment.

As an anti-anthropologist I do not have to concern myself with such matters, and therefore I have much more available freedom. I can allow myself submersion into the experience of the encounter, involving the totality of my being, ready to be transformed in the process. To pass the test of "scientific precision" does not matter to me. I am interested in giving a testimony of *what happens* when we dare take that "mortal leap away from reason" over the barrier of the self with all its history and self-importance.

On one hand there is what could be called "scientific investigation," which can eventually convince other "social scientists" without cause for surprise or pulling rabbits out of the hat. Everything is in order and under control. We scientists understand almost everything, and what we lack, we *will* understand; it is only a question of time. On the other hand there is what can be experienced that does not fit into the purely "tonal"[2] schemes of reason. I believe it is important

---

[2] The rational part of awareness and the perceptual universe linked to it.

that we dare to explore that which does not fit, and make it known.

SCIENTISTS VS. ESOTERICISTS

For a long time two apparently irreconcilable factions, which in essence have many things in common, have dominated the panorama of "indigenous knowledge." In one are found the social scientists with their obsession of searching for proof congruent with the existence of A Single Reality (always in agreement with their ideology or preferred "theoretical framework"). In the other we find many writers who publish tales of "indigenous knowledge" that in most of the cases simply ignore completely the importance of making possible the verification of their tales; therefore we can never be certain if what they tell us is real, fiction, or a combination. The books of the first group are directed toward the academic environment and almost never reach the public at large. Those of the second are directed to a much less demanding public, interested in the spiritual substance of these works, but easygoing when it comes to the reliability of the origin of said tales. Thus the majority of anthropologists fail to have a more human and integrated approach toward indigenous peoples, and those writers whom I will generically label as "esotericists"[3] often fail to seek out sustained contact with real indigenous communities.

In this way, the academics are tied to the coldness of "provable data", and the esotericists allow themselves too many liberties. It is clear that a book is valuable because of what it supplies the reader. Its value does not depend on whether it is a work of literary fiction or a report concerning true facts, but rather on the quality, in form and background, of its message. But the fact that both possibilities are valid

---

[3] I am aware there exist many serious researchers and writers in the esoteric items, but at the other hand, I feel a more critical attitude about their materials is needed.

should not bring authors to mix or confuse one type of literary work with the other, especially without clarifying that fact to their readers.

From my point of view, a novel or an account made into a novel on any theme, including indigenous themes, can be very valuable as long as it has "substance." The content of a novel with substance can be profoundly enriching, it can even motivate us toward a change or a fundamental improvement in our way of living. Why then the fear to accept the magic of literary creation such as it is? Why keep hidden the genius of literary creation as though it had to do with an undesirable personage?

It could be argued that leaving a candle of mystery surrounding the source from which they write gives greater force and credibility to the message of their work, but then we come up to the problem whose consequences in time become more and more serious: the estrangement between indigenous and nonindigenous peoples. We should be clear on this: If we make up our field experiences among indigenous peoples or write novels and present them as containing real facts, we substitute reality for fiction before the eyes of our readers, which tends to encourage admiration for the Indian personages in the books and rejection or indifference toward real Indians.

It is paradoxical that readings concerning the knowledge of Native Americans that have saturated the spiritual literature market of the eighties and the nineties could produce a major alienation toward real Indians. They, after all, do not seem very much like the spectacular Indians from new age fad books, and are scorned by the readers of such books as "inauthentic" or "contaminated" due to colonization. After all, the Indians in the books are more exciting and colorful. Once more, in keeping with custom, the members of the "civilized" culture award themselves the right and the capacity to state the final word regarding the Indians, establishing themselves as judges capable of determining authenticity and ethnic and spiritual purity! This superficial appreciation prevents discovering the true magic found beyond the apparent, and only revealed when, ridding ourselves of prejudice, we open ourselves to direct and sustained contact with that other reality—daily life in the indigenous universe.

We have arrived at a historic moment that demands that we stop and reevaluate our attitude toward indigenous peoples and their knowledge. If we truly want to construct a New Era in which the millennial knowledge of the Indian can help us to ease the emptiness into which we have fallen in modern societies, it is necessary that investigators, writers, readers, and society in general become more demanding and responsible in order to promote an approach between the people of the city and the indigenous peoples who survive preserving their Traditions, Knowledge, and Identity. The pressure on these communities is so great that even a light treatment of these issues could have very serious consequences. To cite just one example—the recent conflicts in the indigenous zones of Chiapas are but the tip of the iceberg, which should cause us to reflect on how far removed we are from real indigenous peoples and the terrible consequences brought about as a result. A small sample will serve to illustrate:

In the middle of 1994 I was giving a lecture on the survival of indigenous knowledge at the dawn of the new millennium when one of those attending asked me about the Indian rebellion in Chiapas against the Mexican government and the political bosses of the region. He wanted to know if I thought the Zapatista rebellion was or was not an "authentic indigenous" movement. When I spoke of the genuinely indigenous nature of the movement, of the marvelous culture and knowledge preserved by these descendants of the Maya, and of the injurious poverty and exploitation to which they are subject, an indignant woman reprimanded me, saying that there was no way the members of the Zapatista army could be Indians. I asked her why she thought that, to which she responded: "If they were true Indians they would not ask for assistance in food and medicine like the Zapatistas are doing, since authentic Indians are too wise to suffer hunger or sickness."

This person, although a bit extreme, exemplifies many others who opt for their own fantasies to the point of rejecting the earth-shaking testimony of reality. But in this case, that attitude can very well mean the difference between life and death for thousands of Indians. Remember that many times the participation or the indifference of society on the whole has been the determining factor in either promoting or halting the annihilation of entire peoples. In annihilation, not only are many human lives lost, but also the marvelous opportunity to enrich the world that we inhabit with a cosmovision so different and so valuable, such as that of the native cultures of the American continent.

Meanwhile, courses on "shamanism" proliferate, allowing us to transform ouselves into shamans in a short time, or we are given access to imitations of rituals that have no effective connection with everyday living and remain empty and inoperative.

So we have, on one hand, the anthropologists; they go to the indigenous communities to test the effectiveness of their theoretical frameworks and to feed their own self-importance as "he or she who is able to understand" the indigenous reality based on intellectual preparation. On the other hand are those consumers of a fantastic indigenous knowledge who seem to be more interested in their books than in getting to know the Indians of flesh and blood. The *true* encounter with the experience and knowledge of the indigenous world continues to be an urgent task in these difficult times, during which we are witnessing the gradual and apparently definitive disappearance of our indigenous face.

Sad panorama. In this moment in our history as a species on this planet—in which we urgently need to find different and more healthy ways to approximate the reality and irreplaceable experience which is life—the physical survival of indigenous peoples who retain much of the Knowledge that we lack, is like a last opportunity to make a true discovery that can result in transformation and growth. This is our golden opportunity—on the verge of disappearing—to have a true encounter with the other, through which we can also discover the *other self* who remains hidden within each one of us.

In my work with indigenous individuals and communities, my intention was not to remain stuck in the immobility of fantasy, nor to become mired in the search for self-confirmation of the field investigator. I have attempted to go as *far* as possible, ready to leave by the wayside the shreds of my own history, of my own ego, of my own description of the world, to thus position myself as *near* as possible to those others who are unknown to us. Whether I have achieved it, at least in part, is not for me to say. I can only contribute the testimony of my efforts.

Although all the events I relate in this book actually occurred, I do not intend to leave out the subjective elements, which I take for granted without difficulty. The subjective is interesting to me because a long time ago I discovered that our experience of reality is *always* subjective, and that "objective" perception is nothing more than a fantasy of reason, since there is no way perception can be produced without the participation of the subject (myself).

On the other hand, I consider that one significant aspect of my work is to serve as a report on something that, in reality, took place. I did not invent it or imagine it; therefore it supplies us with an example of what can be—in concrete reality—an encounter with a form of indigenous knowledge, with living protagonists whose existence can be validated.

FIVE

THE TRADITION OF THE SURVIVING TOLTECS

A LIVING RELIGION

The everyday life of the Wirrarika is involved in every detail with their religious thought. Their religion is not an activity carried out separately, like those who go to church now and then only to forget later everything relating to their supposed faith. For the Wirrarika, religious thought does not consist of a doctrine or a body of beliefs. It is not registered in any kind of sacred book, nor is it administered exclusively by ministers or some authority. Religious authorities who are recognized by all, or who exert some kind of dominion over the community, do not exist. For them religion is a way of life in

which each one of their acts is in relation to the forces govern-
ing the world. As they have no sacred books, organizations, or
religious hierarchies, they share among all the responsibility
to preserve and re-create their cosmogony, day after day, generation after generation. Thus the histories, songs, and legends of Tamatz Kahullumary or Tatewari, or the story of the
creation of the world, are not a closed history. When the
marakame tells the stories, he is not simply repeating something memorized or learned from another sorcerer, rather he is
relating what he is *seeing* in that very moment of the ritual. To
the many stories he has heard during his life concerning the
personages of Wirrarika cosmogony, he will add the stories
that he himself sees or receives directly during those moments
in which his awareness focuses on the *separate reality*.

Among the Wirrarika, the search for God or the Spirit
does not concern things that they tell you about and you
believe. It is a matter of *seeing and listening* for yourself. A
Wirrarika child can listen for many years to the songs and legends of Grandfather Tail of the Deer, or of Tatei Urianaka, but
until he or she sees them personally, he or she will not be truly
initiated into such knowledge. As members of the modern
culture, we too often think that the religious thought of the
Indians is populated with superstitions and imaginary tales.
This is due to the fact that our modern meaning of religion is
exactly that: a body of dogmas we really do not believe, a
body of standards of conduct we do not respect, a series of
stories we never witnessed—empty stories and superstitions,
without any concrete empirical reference. We can speak of
Christ or of God interminably. We can even declare that God
wants this or that, that "he" thinks in such and such a manner,
that "he" behaves thus and so, but we never see "him", nor
does "he" make anything clear that we can affirm.

It is natural that starting from such an empty and poor
religious base, we would think that something similar would
occur among the Indians, if we don't go even further to speak

with petulance of "the primitive religions" and pretend to place ourselves far above them. We make studies and we classify. We make opinions and we believe we understand. The truth is, generally, we have not the slightest idea of what really occurs in the religious experience of the Indians, especially those who preserve the fundamental aspects of the ancient pre-Hispanic religions.

In this sense the Wirrarika are an extraordinary case. Their religion has been preserved practically intact, free from the contamination of the barbaric religions that arrived from Europe starting in the sixteenth century and also those that in more recent times have penetrated our country from the United States.

The word "religion" among them retains its full significance: *religare* is "to reunite," a return to unite humans with the energy that animates the world, which we could call God, Nagual, Spirit, Intent, Iusi[1] or whatever occurs to us.

Precisely because the religious practices and procedures continue to operate among them as an efficient and functional system allowing the men and women of this people to reunite themselves effectively with the Spirit, we can say it is a living religion. It is a true path of return involving complex and unusual handling of perception and awareness; thus, what the marakame relates in his songs are not stories he learned at one point in his life, later to be repeated to the rest. Rather he attains a world or a series of parallel worlds into which he effectively penetrates, at times together with all those present, thanks to the handling of forms of attention the average person does not even suspect exists.

---

[1] The word with which the Wirrarika designate the ultimate energy that sustains everything existing.

THE MARAKAME[2]

Although practically all of the Wirrarika participate in the religious life of their communities, there stands out in this sense the figure of the marakame (they pronounce it mara'ahkame), who, according to anthropologists, is the shaman of the community.

The term *shaman* really doesn't tell us much since it is used to designate—with one pen stroke—all healers, sorcerers, huichol singers, priests, herbalists, dancers, *diableros*,[3] witches, and everything having to do with them, knowing there exist peculiarities relative to each one of such practitioners. The term has been abused so much that now a person can be transformed into a "shaman" through courses lasting a week or so. These are nothing more than refried versions of "Mind Control,"[4] sometimes embellished with indigenous music and even with mind-altering drugs. This kind of imaginary shamanism is especially fashionable in Europe and particularly in Spain.

The case of the marakames should, therefore, be considered apart from the term "shamanism." The marakame is fundamentally the ritual Wirrarika singer, who in his singing transmits the signs for the Grandfather Fire, and refers to the stories of the creation of the world and of the hundreds of personages who populate the Wirrarika cosmogonic universe. He must be present in practically all ceremonious or religious events. The same is true in dealing with propitiating rainfall, or in asking advice about solutions to everyday problems, or in curing a sick person. On such occasions, the marakame enters into a trance and receives instructions directly from the

---

[2] Mara'haa'kame in the Wirrarika language.

[3] A practitioner of black sorcery.

[4] There exist many books on the market about the famous "Silva Mind Control" invented by a Doctor Silva in the United States in the late 1970s.

Powers that govern the world. Singing for one or several nights straight, he relates the designs of the Powers or the unseen reasons that give rise to some illness or the prolongation of a drought.

This is the most simplistic view of what a marakame does. Before I go deeper and refer to more complex tasks of the marakame, it is worth mentioning that there are a great many of them in the mountains. Every small settlement can have one or more. Furthermore, there are no specific requirements to fulfill, nor does it require any authorization except that of the Spirit. There are also women marakames, although they are very few in number, probably due to the demands of gestation and the raising of children.

While it is true that marakames, in general, are self-taught, without instructions, special education, or some teacher who initiates them, we shouldn't therefore think the task is easy or learned quickly (almost all marakames are very old). The task they carry out embodies an astounding degree of complexity in the external—where the number of elements and ritual objects they must handle is impressive—as well as in the internal—where the handling of their attention and perception must be intense enough to "pull" all of those present in the ritual to that other world into which they have entered.

Although I have spent years in direct contact with their rituals, observing and experiencing in my body and my perception the work of the marakame, my conviction grows each time when I realize that what I manage to perceive is but a small part of everything going on. The rituals are extraordinarily rich and complex: everything they do—lighting the fire, dancing, their way of walking, singing, the manner and order in which they seat themselves, their attire, the necessary articles, the work of the ritual singers, the response from the rest, the entrance and exit to the magic circle, the way they approach or address the fire—always has a necessary form, a direction, a rhythm and specific order. Our simplistic image of the ritual, in which the Indians basically dance, sing, and observe the fire, has little to do with reality. Much more occurs, a great deal more! So much goes on that there are rituals that last for days or weeks without repeating the procedures of the day before. It is incredible that *all* the participants perform with concentration and surprising precision, with exact knowledge of how to behave in each moment. As a result, they act as a single body, with complete synchronization, without the intervention of verbal agreements. Curiously, I have never seen a Wirrarika assume the role of "master" and verbally instruct the others.

THE APPRENTICESHIP OF THE SPIRIT

At the beginning I asked myself: How did they learn all this? How is it that no one requires instructions? Silent observation gave me the first part of the answer: They learn since infancy, even from the mother's womb. Maternity and lactation do not exclude women or children from the rituals, not even during the grueling trip to Humun' Kulluaby, so, for literally their entire lives, the Wirrarika participate in the rituals. They learn, participating, without any kind of previous training.

It was among them that I became acquainted with this form of apprenticeship and I continue to regard it as the best, since it doesn't waste time and energy seeking the authorization of reason, the ego, and personal history; rather you are simply placed there, where the situation forces you to act. The second answer—how they move with such precision and synchronization during the rituals—has to do with those concrete links that human awareness is capable of, especially in situations involving high concentration where attention and energy are focused toward a common objective. The result is some type of alignment encompassing the awareness of the participants, and it establishes a form of communication much more subtle and efficient than the ordinary communication of words. The absolute fact is that they are transformed into a single energetic body, which naturally acts in harmonic unity with itself.

Returning to the knowledge of the marakame—although for his entire life he has participated in rituals and observed many marakames, the substantial part of his knowledge is not learned by imitation. Rather he receives directly from the Spirit, who to them appears as the Blue Deer. In fact, it is He who has given these people the task of transforming themselves into marakames; it is not a personal decision.

Having received "the call", they must make many changes, since the way to prepare and to fulfill the "lessons" of Tamatzin is by living an orderly and demanding life, with long periods of abstinence of various kinds, incessant participation in the rituals and concomitant activities, learning to focus the *dreaming* experience in the spiritual apprenticeship, and above all, making the Pilgrimage to Humun' Kulluaby; the home of Tamatz Kahullumary. It is there, in that fundamental *zone of power*, where the marakames and those who are on their way to becoming one, go to search for *their deer*, the fundamental *vision* or *visions* upon which they will construct their task.[5] It is there where they receive the principal parts of their instruction. For this reason, unlike the common Wirrarika who are obligated to make the Pilgrimage to Humun'

---

[5] Don Pedro de Haro, the famous marakame quoted some 25 years ago by Fernando Benitez, told me that in the cosmogony they experience in concrete form, there is not in reality only one deer, but many including the "false deer" who tempts you, dangerously offering power and knowledge, while in actuality it loses you, leading you astray. He also explained to me that in the apprenticeship of the marakame there are five principal deer, which are met one by one, beginning with the smallest and finishing with the discovery of the largest deer: Tamatz Kahullumary. Each deer has its own characteristics and its lessons are relative to the nature of its knowledge, focusing on different aspects of life and awareness.

Kulluaby at least once in their lives, the future marakames, or those already existing as such, have to go many times.

The marakames are as poor as any other Wirrarika, receive no pay for their services, and in addition to their spiritual work, must continue to carry out everyday tasks such as tilling, seeding, and harvesting of their fields, the care of animals, the construction and repair of their dwellings. The reason motivating the Wirrarika to want to transform themselves into marakames surely is nothing else but true spiritual conviction.

A friend of mine commented that after one of his public presentations in Spain, Carlos Castaneda declared that, compared to the members of European modern culture, all Indians are sorcerers. In the case of the Wirrarika this is particularly true, given that almost all of them are expert practitioners of the complex spiritual practices in which they participate from birth, and are therefore capable of handling themselves with efficiency in the everyday world, as well as in the *separate reality* that makes up the world of the *nagual*.

Among the Wirrarika there are many marakames, some better than others, not from a moral point of view, but rather from an energetic one. Some "marakames" are somewhat addicted to drinking, and some have health or survival situations that do not exactly express a high level of energy. It is not a question of judging them because, foregoing considerations aside, all of them lend a valuable and disinterested service to the community. The thing to be aware of is that among the Wirrarika themselves, the levels of knowledge and practice in the spheres of awareness and perception, as well as in the sphere of daily affairs, vary a great deal from person to person.

I have known about fifteen marakames. Among these, I have had a close relationship with four, and I can say that some of them are involved in matters so extraordinary and fascinating that they need add nothing from the stories of Castaneda, which is no overstatement. These marakames, and the more or less secret groups they lead, carry a tremendous responsibility. They must preserve intact, for the generations to come, the body of practices and knowledge dealing with the unsuspected possibilities of awareness and perception, which the indigenous world developed over the centuries and millenniums. That knowledge continues alive and developing, even expanding. As is becoming more apparent, some ramifications of this knowledge are beginning to project themselves outside the Indian world and to touch various receptive spirits. We don't know how far it will go.

INVISIBLE VILLAGES

The Wirrarika live in the most remote and inaccessible regions of the mountains, including the states of Nayarit, Jalisco, and Zacatecas. They live in "towns" that in fact do not exist. I mean by this that if you manage to vanquish all difficulties in order to go to these places—where there exist neither highways, nor dirt roads, nor lights, nor telephone, nor television, nor radio, and the only way to get there is by walking for many hours, sometimes days, without losing your way too much—when finally you arrive at the village of San . . ., you find there is no village! "And where is San . . . ?" you will ask if you have the luck to encounter someone. "Why, it's there right in front of you! Don't you see it . . . ?" "Well, no!"

The Wirrarika do not live grouped together in the place where the center of the community supposedly is, a center generally composed of a ceremonial temple (Kalihuey) and a structure for the meeting of the traditional authorities, plus a few shacks. Rather they live distributed among the ravines and glens of the region. "And where is such and such a fellow's house . . . ?" "Just over there, across the river!" "Very good, many thanks." And then it turns out that the "just over there" takes several hours! Time and distance pass by in another dimension for the Wirrarika. The fact is that each family usually lives quite removed from the others, and they only get together during fiestas. It is then that the religious ceremonies bring them out of their little huts and the "villages" are filled with people.

INACCESSIBILITY

In the Wirrarika communities there live only the Wirrarika. Entry permits for non-Wirrarikas are granted by the local authorities infrequently, generally for representatives of the state government or for representatives of the INI.[6] If outsiders manage to arrive there, and commit the discourtesy of entering the communities without prior consent, they are placed in a jail, called "the stocks." Inside their feet are secured between two enormous planks of wood, with two holes in the middle, so they cannot escape. The time spent in the stocks depends on the mood of "the sheriffs," and the "fine" they will charge the intruders. There have been cases of foreigners held there, after being informed they will be used as "human sacrifices" in the upcoming fiestas. With such jesting, the intruders are ready to leave a fair-sized "voluntary donation" to the community in exchange for their freedom.

THE "FIESTAS"

The religious calendar of the Wirrarika is very full, made up of numerous activities that they simply call fiestas (Neirra): the fiesta of peyote (Hikuri Neirra), the fiesta of tender corn (Tatei Neirra), of the drum (tepo), and the series of ceremonies having to do with the Pilgrimage to Humun' Kulluaby, to name just a few. Of all of them, the most important is the Pilgrimage, which closes the religious calendar of one year and opens the next.

The Pilgrimage to Humun' Kulluaby is carried out year after year. Each community counts on a group responsible for making the trip over the sacred route, the group which goes by the name "jicareros," also known as "peyoteros." They are responsible for organizing the ceremonial activities for the

---

[6] Indigenous National Institute

entire year, and during the Pilgrimage, they carry out the hunt for deer-peyote, gathering large quantities of the sacred cactus, which will be used by the entire community during the months preceding the next Pilgrimage.

HIKURI

Peyote or Hikuri is a fundamental part of the life of the Wirrarika. Practically everyone consumes it from childhood, always in a ritual manner. It is very rare and bad manners when someone "becomes drunk" or misbehaves with peyote. In general they take very small quantities of it, save on very special occasions when it is appropriate to consume large quantities. Existing studies relevant to the subject and my own observations affirm that there exists no kind of physical or mental damage to the Wirrarika due to the use of peyote. On the contrary, they are very sensible, peaceful and, profound people, in their thinking as well as in their way of life.

To return to the Pilgrimage—it is in reality made up of several stages, beginning with the preparation ceremonies, which are carried out in the mountains in each community. Afterward follows a trip of more than four hundred kilometers to the region where the Divine Luminous Tamatz Kahullumary was born, in the desert of San Luis. At different places during the trip, rituals of a high religious significance are carried out, which means the pilgrims take several days to arrive at Humun' Kulluaby. Since the early 1970s, portions of the route have been traversed by bus whenever possible, be it independent transport or in vehicles furnished by the INI. If those are not available, they go on foot the entire way, making the Pilgrimage last about forty days. Usually they take from seven to ten days between leaving and returning to the mountains, where they continue the rituals. Once at Humun' Kulluaby, they carry out the hunt for Hikuri and related rituals. Later they return to the mountains and hunt the deer, which in this case is not deer-peyote but rather real deer. This takes another three to five days. When the hunt is over, they return to the mountains and prepare themselves for the peyote ceremonies, which takes about another week more. In total, they take about one month to celebrate the rituals having to do with the trip to Humun' Kulluaby.

Even though every Wirrarika supposedly should make the Pilgrimage to the Humun' Kulluaby at least one time in his life, some go more and others—who are the exception—never go. The reason they should go at least once is that there, in a direct encounter with Tamatzin, Iusi, or Tatewari, as fortune would have it, the pilgrim will be able to find the answers to the essential questions: Who am I? Where did I come from? Where am I going? What is my task in this life? In particular it is the answer to this last question that determines whether Wirrarika dedicate themselves to the fields, to business, to healing, to ritual singing, to the playing or fabrication of musical instruments, or to any kind of undertaking to change their lives. There have been Wirrarika who find themselves in countries far removed from the scene—such as Cuba or in Europe, precisely because in Humun' Kulluaby they received the message to travel there. This is why the Wirrarika are great travelers, or to put it colloquially—very wayward. In effect, those who wish to go far in Knowledge must realize part of their apprenticeship outside their world of origin, to which they almost always return.

Those who go on Pilgramage more often are motivated by some special urgency such as to solicit favors from the Powers that govern the world, to resolve very serious problems, or to give thanks for these same favors. Also they search for clarity in dealing with problems or decisions they are not sure how to resolve. In any case, those who go most often to Humun' Kulluaby are those preparing to be marakames or functioning as such, as I mentioned before. There is also the group of pilgrims who deserve separate consideration: the jicareros.

THE JICAREROS

The jicareros are a closed group of Wirrarika who, during a period of five years, have the enormous responsibility of organizing all the religious activities of the community. These include carrying out the yearly Pilgrimage to the desert of Humun' Kulluaby and other sacred sites. Each community has it own group of jicareros who organize and carry out their activities independently, although in general they coincide in the dates and types of ceremonies. The group numbers more than fifteen and less than thirty members in addition to the marakame who is their natural leader. As in each community there are many marakames, jicareros look to the most powerful to carry out their task. There are many duties, which they maintain during their entire stay in the group. Thus, there is the urukuakame—he who leads the way during journeys and he who indicates the way to follow. Many times this duty is filled by the oldest man. Every one of these duties is related to one of the sacred entities, so that apart from his normal name, each one will adopt that of one of the original powers who formed the world and determined the function of everything: Tatewari[7], Tayau[8], Kahullumary[9], Urianaka[10]. The one who marches always ahead of the marakame, walking in front of him on journeys, and the person in charge of taking care of the power objects that the ritual singer will utilize in the ceremonies, is called naurratame. Each name has its significance

---

[7] the Grandfather Fire

[8] the Sun, also called Tau, Taveviekame or Tave'errika

[9] In the beginning of time, Kahullumary, the possessor of the Book of Knowledge, transformed himself into a deer and offered himself to be hunted in the ritual hunt, which gave rise to the sacred hunt of the deer the Wirrarika carry out as part of the Pilgrimage to Humun' Kulluaby.

[10] Earth

and its history, also its specific corresponding activities within the ritual activities of the group.

After five years, the jicareros will hand over the responsibility to the new jicareros who will be responsible for the next cycle. The majority of the new jicareros fulfill their duties of their own will, though some are assigned as an obligation. For the majority, to belong to the select group is a privileged opportunity to live much closer to the Spirit. Some of them, upon completing their five-year cycle, join the new group of jicareros or continue working very close to "their" marakame, who is also relieved every five years. Even those who have been chosen "by force," in a short time find a spiritual family among their companions with whom they end up feeling very close.

Inside the Wirrarika community, the jicareros are a separate group, due to the fact that they live, full time, concerned with matters of the Spirit. Their meeting center is the ceremonial Kalihuey, called *tukipa* in their own tongue, where there must always be a fire burning, since Tatewari is the principal deity and he is considered the first and most ancient of the powers, predating even the great-grandfather tail of the deer.

The jicareros travel a lot because the sacred territory of the Wirrarika is very large, including not only the desert of San Luis Potosi (Humun' Kulluaby), but also the sacred places in the state of Durango (Haurra-manaka), Lake Chapala (Rapaviyame), the ocean of Nayarit (Tatei Aramara), a lady of the waters (Tatei Matinieri),[11] and the famous Tehotihuacan as well, the cradle of Toltequity. They must bring offerings every year to all these sites and celebrate the corresponding rituals in each. None of this excuses them from the multiple responsibilities of everyday survival, such as planting and harvesting.

---

[11] who also dwells in a spring in the San Luis desert

They receive no salary; on the contrary, all these journeys, their preparations and the elements involved in the ritual run up costs that the jicareros pay out of their own pockets, often empty like those of the rest of the Wirrarika. Of all the jicareros, the one who works most and travels most is the marakame. While the jicareros can share the multiple errands among themselves and, on some occasions, not all of them make the trip to the sacred sites, the marakame must be present at all times, since without him the rituals could not be carried out.

The name "jicareros" appears to have come from a time long ago. I have considered a possible relation between this name and the fact that they collect peyote, that is, Hikuri or Hikuli. In the writings of Lumholtz, at the end of the last century, he calls them "hikuleros,"[12] which looks like jicareros, although he evidently did not enter into their activities, since he does not contribute anything in that respect. This possible relation is supported by the fact that in the present day they also are commonly called peyoteros. The former notwithstanding, this was the answer I received when I asked my teokaris (brothers, companions) jicareros the meaning of their name:

"Hey, Tayau, why do you call yourselves jicareros?"

"Uuuh, that comes from a long time ago! Look. We are a group. We are called jicareros because we keep the tradition. Not only out of preference, but out of obligation, so it won't be lost, because the day the custom ends, the Tradition, then we Wirrarika are likewise finished, as if they had given us poison! So, since we keep the tradition, then all together we are that, the 'jícara'[13] of God. In that cup are kept Knowledge and the

---

[12] See *El Mexico Desconcido*, Carl Lumholtz, published in Mexico by the Indigenous National Institute. (Its first publication dates from 1890.)

[13] Jicara is a kind of bowl used in indigenous towns of Mexico for keeping food or for keeping ritual objects.

most important customs of our great-great-grandfathers!"[14]

Before beginning my tale about the Pilgrimage to Humun' Kulluaby, I must comment about the community in whose group of jicareros I have been participating and with whom I made the Pilgrimage.

Santa Maria[15] is a Wirrarika community hemmed in by the most inaccessible parts of the mountains, a zone of deep gorges and high mountains, which receives, on very rare occasions, visitors from the outside. If the Wirrarika communities have kept themselves isolated by their geography and their customs, Santa Maria is the best example of both, since it is physically the most inaccessible and the restrictions having to do with the entry of outsiders are tough. In this it is distinguished from the other communities in which the presence of visitors is not so unusual, for matters having to do with the commerce of artisans, or for being accessible from the dirt roads coming from Zacatecas, as occurs, for example in San Andres Cohamiata. It is in Santa Maria where the preservation of the traditions has been kept most orthodox and almost without contamination. But the special significance of Santa Maria is due not only to its location. In some way it is the center of the Wirrarika spiritual universe, since it was there that Tatewari was supposedly born, the equivalent of saying that it

---

[14] It never ceases to be interesting, this relation between the name "jicarero" and the word "jicara", which is a Náhuatl word. The word has as roots, "xictli" (navel) and "cali" (house) implying the house or the enclosure of the navel, which in pre-Hispanic cosmogony has a sacred significance. The navel was the center, the point of contact with the Cosmos. Thus they spoke of the navel of the world, or the navel of the moon (Mexico), and the physical and celestial geography of the pre-Hispanic world was full of xicltlis (navels). Therefore, a "jicara" was not just any receptacle, but rather a container used only to keep sacred things in. In that regard I recommend consulting the works of Gutierre Tibon, *Historia del nombre y fundacion de la ciudad de Mexico*, and *El ombligo como centro cosmico*, published by the Fondo de Cultura Economica, Mexico.

[15] A fictitious name to protect the privacy of the community and to avoid their being disturbed.

is the center of their cosmogony. This is made manifest by the fact that the Wirrarika of other communities on occasion undertake a journey to Santa Maria, which then itself becomes a destination for spiritual pilgrims to "make an offering" or to seek approval or advice from one of the Powers of the world.

It was in this community, center of history and cosmogony of the Wirrarika people, where I encountered the clearest and most powerful expression of the surviving Toltequity: the magic universe of the Wirrarika.

PART
THREE

EXPERIENCES
IN THE
TOLTECS'
WORLD

SIX

ANTI-
ANTHROPOLOGY
IN
ACTION

What follows are examples of field work relating to some of my experiences among the Wirrarika. (See the color insert for some photos of these experiences.) I will not attempt to relate a complete history of my fifteen-year relationship with that world, but just simply reveal some typical moments of my experience among them that are congruent with the objective of the present work. My intentions are not academic, or to make a comprehensive study, or even to portray a likeness of Wirrarika culture. This is only a personal testimony that will show some of the features of their unusual way of being and living, and the "anti-anthropological" way in which I have approached them.

During the period of my first contact with the Wirrarika, I was actually studying anthropology, but at that time it was already quite clear to me that academic anthropology and its theoretical frameworks had little to offer in the search for my Spirit. From the time of my experiences with the Náhuas, I began to incorporate the traits of anti-anthropology, which would characterize all my doings among the Indians. My encounter with the Wirrarika was, from the beginning, motivated by my own internal restlessness. I did not go to study them, or to gather folkloric or exotic experiences, but in search of suitable channels for my urgencies of internal growth. I wanted to learn and—above all—experience for myself and in myself, those other forms of knowledge ignored by modern people, which indigenous peoples such as these have jealously preserved through the centuries and millennia.

Diverse works and studies about the Wirrarika, with different levels of depth and accomplishment, have presented to the Western world the principal traits of their culture. The majority of these studies represent very respectable efforts, considering everything the investigators had to do to carry them out. They invested much time and work to arrive at very inaccessible places, to obtain informants, to do interviews and recordings, to find translators, and then to write their reports.

The works of Lumholtz[1] at the end of the nineteenth century are amazing for the degree of openness and curiosity they reflect on the part of the investigator. They were written during an era in which the ontological "inferiority" of the Indians was regarded as obvious, therefore not even discussed. Also investigators such as Furst, Zing, and Benitez[2] contributed their efforts at knowing the Wirrarika way of life and thought.

---

[1] See *El Mexico Desconocido*, mentioned on pg. 63.

[2] See *Mitos y Arte Huicholes*, Peter Furst and Salomon Nahmad, Coleccion SEP 70s, no. 50, Mexico City, 1972.

See *Los Huicholes: Una Tribu de Artistas*, Robert M. Zing, *Colección Clásicos de la Antropologia Mexicana*, Instituto Nacional Indigenista, Mexico City, 1982.

See *Los Indios de Mexico*, Fernando Benitez, Ediciones Era, Mexico City, 1976.

In spite of the seriousness of such work, the majority of investigators who approach the indigenous universe have been—with the best of intentions—external observers, not participants in the world they wanted to know. Such external observation is not considered negative by academics. They share the belief of all rationalist Western culture that it is not necessary to experience something in order to know it; it is enough to observe, rationalize, register, and classify it. In the case of ethnologists, there is also an entire series of theoretical frameworks, which supposedly aids them in understanding the reality of the "ethnologized." They start from the basis that there is only one reality and that the point of view of Western science is the most correct one possible. Such a supposition discards the possibility that there are aspects of reality that cannot be detected by simple external and rationalist observation.

One of the most common failings of the anthropologist is the same as that of modern people in general: We believe that what we perceive is the totality of what is occurring in the scene we are observing. Thus, when witnessing a ritual, we observe indigenous people in a sitting position with their heads between their knees, we could say: "After the dances, the members of the group appeared very tired and they sat down to rest," without noticing that those people, far from finding themselves tired, might be engaged in very intense work on a level of reality that we do not even suspect. In our arrogance, we accept as a fact that what we do not see, simply does not exist. Anthropologists formulate their explanations, discourses, and theories, basing them on what they saw and how they interpreted it, regarding it as a fact that things are exactly thus. However, they do not take into account what they overlooked—the Indian informants respond only to the questions asked and Westerners generally do not know how to pose the proper questions relating to the fundamental points of the cosmovision they seek to understand. As a result, the conversation will revolve around those points they believe to be important, rather than necessarily touching upon the real fundamental aspects of the indigenous universe. To complicate the situation even more, many Indians, particularly those most deeply involved in spiritual matters, are experts in telling nosy foreigners exactly what they want to hear, knowing they'll be rid of the outsiders that much sooner.

So, in spite of great and sincere efforts, the works and reports about the indigenous universe by expert anthropologists are basically "disconnected" from the internal happenings of that universe, although they have never realized it. They were there, they asked all the questions, they saw it with their own eyes, but they were never aware of what was really going on, they never found out that they were not aware. Interpretations from the point of view of Western thought cannot show us more than reflections of the very same Western thought projected toward the exterior and then taken as reality.

Investigators who do not participate with the totality of their being, who do not transform themselves into the *other*, cannot perceive the *otherness* passing in front of their eyes. They only look at themselves and their own world, without realizing that through their interpretations and their observation disconnected from the *other*, they are inventing a world that does not attain the characteristics of the indigenous universe, but rather their own universe: the universe of modern Western culture.

For them to penetrate into the perception of that other world, they have to detach themselves from their own ego, from their own history, from their own name, in order to change and merge themselves in the encounter with the others. Only in this way can they free themselves from the mirror that traps their perception, that normally reflects their ideas about the world—always taken as the only reality.

The difficulty for investigators in overcoming the *barrier of perception* is that they find themselves trapped in a very particular way of perceiving that has as its permanent reference the description of the world they learned from other members of their society starting at a very early age. This apprenticeship assumes the role of constructing by itself that learned description, which they take as the only reality, while at the same time remaining unaware that this description is projecting that reality from inside themselves onto the beings and things making up the external world. In this sense a sorcerer, accustomed to conceiving the world as a space in which there coexist multiple realities, has the advantage. Thus, the Indians who allude to aspects of reality that violate the logic of the everyday world have not lost their judgment, nor are they ignorant or superstitious, rather they have learned by experience that to different realities also belongs different logic. A man of knowledge or a sorcerer can even be an expert in the movement and eventual integration of both worlds.

The foundation of my work over the years, among indigenous peoples as well as encounter groups I have coordinated, has been the insistence on learning to jump, time and time again and in multiple mediums, through the *barrier of perception*. We learn to penetrate the separate reality, which opens itself to our experience when we can detach ourselves from the reflection of ourselves and our world of personal history and self-importance. Because I have been able to make those jumps, I can affirm the existence of the other world. Its perception reveals to us the hidden nature of the indigenous world and of the world in general, which embraces at once the everyday and the extraordinary. Penetrating into the separate reality places before us both the amazing phenomena that can take place during the experience of a magic ritual or ceremony among the Indians, and those much more enriching alternative realities underlying our interpersonal relationships, in our intimate world, or in our field of work. Thus it is that our everyday world also contains its own separate reality, its own parallel worlds, although we do not suspect it.

Free from the neurotic fantasies that insist on looking for absolute truths, I aspire only to present a simple testimony of what occurred in that indigenous world, of what I saw and what I did among these people whose time in history we still have the privilege to share. Right now, as I write this, they are alive, on the same planet as ourselves, in this same instant, carrying out their ceremonies and rituals to contact the Spirit, the same way and with the same objectives as their ancestors, the ancient Toltecs, practiced millennia ago.

From all my work with the indigenous peoples of Toltec descent, I am taking—as examples—three experiences that can be regarded as three moments of my integration with their world and of my development as a human being. These moments represent neither the beginning nor the end of my work among them. The first is an initial approximation that portends some intuitively anti-anthropological features. The second is a moment of transition in which my intention of penetrating into the magic world of the Indian is clear and expresses itself through actions and continuing tasks. It is like knocking on an invisible door using the force of my acts. The third is the moment in which the door opens and finally I achieve a perception in common with those beings who make up the mysterious world, for which I had searched so long and which so long eluded me.

Of the three excerpts, the first comes from my time as a student of anthropology; therefore the style is more formal and less natural than in the two following, there being almost ten years intervening between it and the following stages. I included it because it serves to illustrate the very different way I saw things as I transformed my attitude into an approximation of the *others*.

These are three passages about my adventures in the peculiar world of the best representatives of surviving Toltequity: the Wirrarika.

SEVEN

ECLIPSE
IN
LA' UNARRE[1]

[2] The following religious phenomenon I will attempt to describe is one of many manifestations of this order displayed by the Wirrarika. For this ethnic group, like many in Mexico, practically their whole life is a sacred act since it is tied almost entirely to their myths. In spite of the many changes that history has imposed on their way of life, they have been able to preserve, through unrelenting resistance, the general structure of their ancestral tradition. This can be observed in the

---

[1] Wirrarika name for the Sacred Mountain, also known as the "Palace of the Governor" (the Sun).

[2] This text was originally written as a field report during the beginning of my studies at the School of Anthropology. I have tried to preserve the style and original form to thus reflect the perception I had at that time of the Wirrarika, although later I would discover some erroneous interpretations and would know the significance of many details that originally escaped me.

75

sacredness they impose on everything they do, to such a degree that even those elements of modern civilization that they sparingly incorporate into their way of life have been integrated within the general feeling of their culture.

The present work is the description of a peyote ceremony (called "Hikuri" in the indigenous tongue) that I had the fortune to witness as a participating observer. It is necessary to clarify that I had had no previous studies that would have given me a moderate understanding (in ethnological terms) of the phenomenon I observed. For this same reason, the field investigation dealing with the phenomenon in question was not as profound (from the academic point of view) as it could have been had I known I was going to witness an event worthy of ethnographic work. Therefore, I propose this work be considered simply as a nonprofessional description by a novice observer on the terrain of scientific anthropology, which places us closer to the common humanist view than the viewpoint of the prepared anthropologist. In this sense, the value of this description could be in the sincerity and the spontaneity of the observer.

On the other hand, not having great knowledge of the phenomenon I witnessed placed me in a position of receptivity, which I perhaps would not have achieved had I arrived "knowing what I was going to see." That very ignorance put me in a condition to ascertain what I could of the phenomenon directly from the Wirrarika, which might have resulted in a closer understanding of reality from the viewpoint of the indigenous people themselves. My situation as a beginning anthropologist, without a specific plan of study, was similar to that of Cultural Relativism.

I was visiting with two friends in the former rich mining town, today the virtual ghost town of Real de Catorce, in the state of San Luis Potosi. When the ore was exhausted, work ceased, the large houses and estates were abandoned and vegetation gradually took over, transforming them into relics without a roof, reminders of a prosperous era that is no more.

This town was established in what for thousands of years was, and still today continues to be, the sacred region for the Wirrarika people: Humun' Kulluaby, the region where the luminous divinity, The Deer-Peyote, was born.

For this reason and in accordance with their cosmovision, the Wirrarika make a Pilgrimage year after year in the semi-desert of San Luis Potosi. The few residents of the town occasionally observe the arrival of compact groups of Wirrarika on their way to Humun' Kulluaby. For me and my two friends, students of anthropology, to encounter one of these groups signified an event worthy of our attention. We had just arrived in town and were eating in a restaurant when in came an Indian whom we could recognize by his exquisite attire characteristic of the Wirrarika. He quietly slipped away toward the back part of the restaurant. We, intrigued, asked our waitress, with whom we had been conversing, who he was and what he was doing there.

The question did not seem to surprise her; our conversation had revolved around anthropological questions and our interest in approaching different social groups of our country. She said he was called Pedro[3] and he was a Wirrarika on a Pilgrimage. Pedro and other members of his community had passed several times through Real de Catorce where he had come into contact with the owner of the restaurant, who offered to periodically buy some of the artwork they crafted and whose sale would help them to subsist. The agreement was that the owner would supply the material and pay them for the labor, then later sell the product in a shop for a far higher price.

Pedro was very eloquent, blessed with a disposition and an expressive capacity that contradicted the classic view of the Indian as a humble type unsure of himself. In the several encounters we had with him, he became what seemed like an

---

[3] In this part, as in the entire book, the names are changed to preserve the privacy of the persons and the communities.

"informant"—but more than anything else, he became our friend. It was he who introduced us a little into the vision of the Wirrarika world, which we found functioning to a surprising degree. Also it was he who allowed us to attend the ceremony that motivated this work.

Contrary to what misinformed people of the city are accustomed to think, Indians do not regard white people as superior beings, rather they tolerate and treat us with patience. Their attitude is: The whites and the Mexicans are crazy, they do not respect the sacredness of the world and are sick for money and desire for property. They are dangerously crazy, since they have the power to cause problems, which is what they normally do. Far from being arbitrary, these observations were made during several conversations we had with the Wirrarika from Pedro's group, which was made up of a variety of men and women who spoke Spanish. Almost always they spoke in their own language, avoiding Spanish even in front of mestizos and whites. However, with us, they were always courteous and we were able to establish a good communication.

We noticed that the males treated their women very affectionately. The women did not appear to be subordinated, rather they were listened to, attended to, and were participants in the affairs of the community. We also noticed the care and love which they all devoted to the children, especially the smallest.

We observed also a notable cohesion within the group. We had the impression that this cohesion had its basis in the cosmovision of the group which, in their own words was oriented toward "an orderly life, walking straight." I want to underline the fact that we remained strongly impressed by the congruence they demonstrated in their way of life and their spiritual conceptions, which they expressed more with their actions than with their words. The quality and moral force they displayed reaffirmed that we, members of the Western "super culture," have much to learn from the cultures mistakenly called "primitive." During the ceremony, we could observe that the Wirrarika were an ethnic group very proud of their traditions.

NARRATION OF THE PEYOTE CEREMONY

We arrived at the semi-destroyed building where the group of Wirrarika were lodged about 6:30 a.m. Pedro had told us "at dawn." We found them awake and conversing. There were eighteen members originating from different settlements in the mountains of Jalisco. The group was formed in the following manner:

Huicho was the oldest. In spite of the fact that his wrinkles denoted an age greater than sixty years, his body was strong, his movements agile, and his dress was quite humble, although in the Wirrarika mode. He was the marakame of the group. In his daily life he was a very calm and peaceful man and he spoke little. He worked the same as the rest in making hand woven apparel while they were in Real de Catorce, and in the field when they were in the mountains. He went about accompanied by his wife, a woman also of advanced age, and by Guadalupe, his son, a likable and lively boy around twelve or thirteen years of age, who participated in the same activities as the rest.

Very close to Huicho was Vicente, a young Wirrarika of perhaps twenty-five years. In the beginning we thought he was a somewhat "culturated" member of the community, given that his dress was not Wirrarika but rather mestizo: khaki pants, plaid shirt, jacket, and boots (all the rest wore huaraches[4] made from tires). Later, we discovered that to have been a hasty appraisal, since Vicente behaved in everything like a Wirrarika. He knew every step of the ritual and participated actively in it. Really the only appreciable difference was the clothing.

---

[4] sandals with a rubber sole made from old tires (the originals were made with a vegetable sole)

Then there was Pedro. It was he we became closest to and with whom we conversed the most. His clothing was very complete, incorporating practically all the elements of Wirrarika dress. Nevertheless, his poverty level was undifferentiated from the rest. He was much younger than Huicho and he was also a shaman. Although he was not a marakame, he was the second huichol singer and he knew how to heal. As is usual among them, he inherited this knowledge from his father who was a singer and who put Pedro as a small child on the path "little by little, every year a step. Yes, life is like a ladder. Reaching up to God; but you have to work a lot, think, think, because God speaks to you, He speaks to you always. Only we don't stop to listen!" "You people have one God. Mmmmhh, poor things! We have many! therefore, we are never alone!" "God is in everything: in the earth, in the plants, in the animals, in the water, in the people. That's why we love everything—everything—and everything takes care of us. Ah, and then the whites tell us no! That the earth is not alive, that the clouds are not alive. Hence, if the earth is not alive, if the clouds are not alive, then how does it rain so the corn can grow tall and beautiful (!) keeping us alive? So, how can they give us life if they are not alive?"

Pedro was accompanied by his son, a child of about five years. There was also Hilario, Pedro's brother, about his age, but we gathered a little younger, since Pedro's authority over him was noticeable, although their relation was very cordial and affectionate. Hilario was quite a tall and thin Indian. He dressed like a poor mestizo, but he carried in his hat the feathers typical of the Wirrarika, "the Spirit." He was a very quiet man with a big smile; he gave the complete image of the good man (we could not describe him any other way), always in good humor, always with good advice. "No, you shouldn't go around with women like that, for what? What good does it do you to go with one and then another if you don't learn to love? Look at me and my woman, we were married when I was fifteen. Many years have passed and here we are together, so peaceful and content. I don't go with other women. She respects me and we love each other. Maybe you think she is not very beautiful, but we have learned to love one another and that for me is as though she were the most beautiful of all." Hilario was accompanied by his wife, who seemed a little older than he. They treated each other with affection. They had a son of hardly a year and a half who, nevertheless, surprised us a great deal since at his young age he already manifested an autonomy and confidence unusual in children of the same age. He was always playing, climbing up on piles of wood. He knew several songs in Wirrarika and some others in Spanish, as he understood both languages, although the language he spoke most was Wirrarika. He was a very friendly child in spite of the fact we were strange and "Mexican."

Next was Cirilo, who spent most of the time in the mountains and also periods in Mexico City where he went to sell his arts and crafts. He was the most heavy set of the group, without being really fat. He was about thirty years old and he dressed in complete Wirrarika attire. His clothes were the most richly embroidered, perhaps due to his business in the capital. He was, without doubt, the humorist of the group, the one who made the rest of them laugh the most, even though every Wirrarika was a master of humor. Later we would discover that his role was of great importance in the peyote rituals. Cirilo was accompanied by his wife, a young woman, maybe eighteen years old, exceedingly beautiful. Her facial features were totally indigenous and could compete advantageously with any beauty from the city. She also was dressed in clothes that could be considered the best of the Wirrarika repertoire. They carried with them a child perhaps six months old, which the woman always had with her, using a shawl to carry him on her back thus keeping her hands free for working.

There were also four small children, already able to walk, whose paternity we could not discern, since all the adults equally took care of them.

Lastly there was Tomás, a man we would consider perhaps the most enigmatic of the group. Tomás's expression was grave and silent most of the time, in spite of the fact that we observed him laughing on occasion. He seemed to be very close to Pedro.

To our surprise, we found the owner of the restaurant there as well ("the boss") and some of his friends of foreign origin who were noisy and displayed a false attitude of respect toward the Indians, more interested in their own addictions than in anything else. This was quite disagreeable to us, since we already felt ourselves intruding a little in attending a ritual of these men and women who have been suffering the hostile social-cultural pounding of the West for several centuries. Nevertheless, we observed the Wirrarika acting as if these people did not exist. They did not seem bothered by their presence; they simply ignored them completely, even pretending not to understand Spanish when these people spoke to them. The owner they treated with enough consideration although also with a little coldness. (On one occasion Pedro confessed to us that they knew the owner was robbing them with the amount he was paying them for their labor, since they knew at what price he sold their products in turn, but there was nothing they could do as they had no capital with which to buy the raw materials themselves.) We observed that the uncouth presence of these foreigners did not alter the course of the ceremony since the Wirrarika knew, with complete subtlety, how to "keep them behind the line." As it turned out, in the nocturnal phase, which lasted all night, these "interested observers" seemed to lose interest and they fell asleep.

It was the morning of the 30th of May. We did not know the purpose of the ceremony that we were to attend. Later we were informed by Pedro that it was a ceremony for the birth of the Sun: "When the new Sun is born, everything is new, everything begins again, but is different." We left the ruined mansion about 6:45 a.m. and we began to walk toward the mountains, in the direction of the most sacred place for the Wirrarika after Humun' Kulluaby: the sacred summit, La' Unarre.

The Wirrarika walked in silence, single file. Their pace was swift and quiet. Soon Real de Minas remained behind, and the road became a stony path surrounded by green fields of grass (we found later that most of the year these mountains are dry). There was a dense fog covering the mountains, and the silhouette of the pilgrims outlined against them produced an effect that, to our eyes, evoked millennial traditions, making us think of the thousands of people who, for centuries, had visited this place with similar intentions: "to encounter and propitiate the forces that rule the destiny of humans."

As time went on and the group advanced, the fog began to disperse and the sun came out. We arrived at the summit of a mountain and walked along a small ridge, skirting chasms and ravines. When we had been climbing for about an hour, the Wirrarika decided to stop since "the owner's group had fallen behind and they could become lost." To our displeasure, we had to wait for them. While the whites arrived out of breath, the Wirrarika conversed. After a brief rest (for the blond ones), we continued on our way. The foreigners again fell behind, but now we did not wait for them and they had to return by themselves. At one point on the way, we arrived at a small pond that was very significant to the Wirrarika. They became very content. Pedro took out a small bottle from his handbag and filled it with water from the pond after drinking a little. We asked him if it was good to drink. "Uuuh, why not! It's very good. You take a little, put it in your house and it takes care of you! Water corn with it and it grows huge, beautiful!" With some trepidation we drank the sacred water to quench our thirst and had no problems with it; quite the contrary, we felt very well.

Just before arriving at the summit of the Sacred Mountain,

the men began to gather some dry trunks of maguey and we decided to help. Later we would learn that these logs were for feeding Tatewari (the Grandfather Fire). At the summit of the Mountain, the spectacle was impressive, especially for the Wirrarika: We were looking at the land where the Luminous Divinity, Humun' Kulluaby was born. We found ourselves on the highest point of the mountain range; below was an enormous desert valley, the place where the Wirrarika made their pilgrimages every year to carry out the hunt for the Deer-Peyote. The view from this height was magnificent.

After contemplating for a while, the Wirrarika went into action again. It was about ten o'clock in the morning. Huicho and Pedro organized themselves to give life to Tatewari. While the fire was coming to life, Huicho began to sing. Once the fire was going, the sun began to hide—an annular eclipse of the sun was taking place! The air turned cold and the fire stood out more in the twilight. Pedro began to sing another text in something that seemed like a canon. Huicho had not yet finished his song when Pedro began singing his and so on successively.

Meanwhile, with devotion the rest placed the food they had brought for Tatewari. They placed a shawl on the ground and filled it with objects, transforming it into an altar. Upon it they arranged chocolate, cookies, *tejuino* (a fermented drink made from corn, which the Wirrarika prepare), a yarn painting representing deer figures, peyote, corn, and the sun, in very stylized forms whose meaning we were unable to comprehend. By the time the altar was ready, the eclipse was total. Huicho and Pedro had in each hand *muvieri* (small staffs with colored feathers, sometimes with a squirrel tail, containing the power of the shaman) that moved in time with their singing. Their singing, without being a chorus, maintained a very intense correlation. It produced in us an overwhelming sensation in spite of not understanding what they were singing, since in no part of the ritual did they use a word of Spanish.

We found ourselves around the fire. The twilight in the middle of the day lent a dramatic effect to the lighting of candles, which took place at that moment. We too had lighted candles in our hands. The cookies were placed in a metal container and sprinkled with water from a sacred site, then passed out to everyone. The procedure was as follows: The container was passed to one of the members who received it with reverence. The person made a series of movements with it first, as though toasting the cardinal points, and then straight up. He or she took a cookie and after eating it, passed the container to another person and so on successively. Some of the Wirrarika uttered words in their tongue while making the indicated movements. The singing of the marakame Huicho and Pedro continued practically without pause during the entire ceremony, which lasted about an hour, except when they were arranging or preparing some of the material elements of the ritual.

It was clearly impossible for us to penetrate into the profound meaning of the ritual. We did not understand the language they used, but also the Wirrarika prepare themselves from the time they are very small to be able to participate in the ceremonies with the required devotion and precision. The dramatic effect that each step of the ritual inspired in the participants was manifest in their expressions as well as in their level of concentration.

Once the ceremony on the Sacred Mountain was completed, they began to collect some of the elements on the altar— the yarn painting and the metal container, but they left the offerings of the cookies, chocolate, and tejuino in the fire. We were surprised at the facility the Wirrarika had for changing their state of being on a moment's notice. Hardly had they finished the ceremony, which had been very intense, when they became joyful and humorous. Later we would verify that this apparent change of attitude was not what it seemed. Although they were smiling on the outside, they had inside a feeling of sacredness that was the result of ritual practices in which they themselves were made sacred. We would have required a much more extensive field study to determine to what point they maintained that attitude during their everyday life in the mountains.

We descended the mountain by more or less the same route we took climbing up. At the halfway point, we stopped for about ten minutes. We were chatting quietly and Cirilo brought out a melon, which somehow he managed to divide among all those present. Later, from his same handbag (anyone would be surprised to see the great quantity of items the Wirrarika carry in their handbags), he removed a bottle of tequila, opened it, and passed it to Pedro. Pedro stood up to receive it. He removed the small staff with feathers he carried on his hat, and while inserting one of the feathers into the bottle and casting a few drops toward each of the cardinal directions, he uttered a series of words aloud with a force that took us by surprise. The maneuver was spectacular for its suddenness and above all, for the power and conviction of his voice. After performing the action, he took a drink and passed the bottle to the rest. Each one of the Wirrarika wetted a finger upon receiving the bottle, cast a few drops toward the cardinal points as well as straight up, and then took only one drink. Later we would observe that this action was carried out every time they took a drink. We asked Pedro the reason for the procedure, to which he responded: "When one is going to drink, before doing so, he offers some first to God so He will take care of him. If not, he drinks too much, gets drunk, loses himself and soon he is fighting, losing his money, or getting into trouble; on the other hand, this way God tells him He will watch over him and then he is at ease."

We continued on our course until we arrived at Real, again at the "house" where the Wirrarika lodged. This was in the ruins of an abandoned house where they lived and worked during their stay in Real. Upon entering, we found ourselves in the patio around which were located different rooms, the majority without a roof. The patio also had no roof. The ground was of trodden earth and there were a few wooden beams they used for seating. There they were going to carry out, this very night, a peyote ceremony that would be a continuation of the rites they began on La' Unarre.

Pedro told us they were going to have a fiesta. "We are going to play the little guitar, to dance, and sing all night." With such a general description, we were left with the idea they were going to have an ordinary party to have fun. Later we would see it was something very different. At this point, after having been around them for some days, we treated the Wirrarika with a certain amount of familiarity and they likewise with us. We were friendly especially with Pedro and his brother Hilario with whom we often spoke, and they answered our questions. About twelve noon we departed, promising Pedro to return in the evening.

HIKURI NEIRRA

It was around eight in the evening when we returned to "the house of the Wirrarika." We found them lighting a fire in the center of the patio and making preparations for "the fiesta." The group of foreigners we had seen in the morning were there. They were very joyful, joking and singing noisily. They were young Europeans of the type who travel with little money and whose slovenly appearance, long hair, and a liking for drugs, earned them the loose title of "hippies." Perhaps it was because they were noisy, or for some other reason that Huicho, in spite of being generally quiet and humble, asked them to leave. He spoke to them softly, trying not to appear discourteous. We looked on, wondering whether he was referring to us as well.

He explained to them that they were going to have a fiesta that was for no one but the Wirrarika, that it was their custom and that outsiders could not remain; that the Wirrarika were not going to sleep and it would be very boring for the foreigners. He rejected all appeals from them and they finally drifted away. We had taken refuge in the part of the house belonging to Hilario and his family. When we asked him, he told us we could stay, since Pedro had invited us. He also explained that when we had gone out earlier, the foreigners had remained there all day. They had been drinking, singing, and smoking marijuana. The Wirrarika did not know how to get rid of them. When it was time for the ceremony, there was no other solution than for Huicho to tell them directly.

Once tranquillity was restored, the Wirrarika continued with their preparations. They placed around the fire different elements. First were two *ekipales*, chairs made of a material similar to reed, covered with deer skin, with an antler from the same animal, which served to support the back of the chair against the ground. These ekipales were sacred elements to the Wirrarika; they used them for ceremonies and only the marakame or, on occasion, one of the helpers, was allowed to sit in them. They also placed a pair of metal chairs where the musicians would sit. On the other side of the fire, directly across from the marakame's chair, was placed a yarn painting similar to the one used in the morning, only the drawings were different: This had in the center a campfire out of which came something like little worms, which represented Tatewari speaking to the Wirrarika. There also appeared ears of corn and symbols of peyote, as well as arrows and several figures in intense colors. Under the yarn painting they placed objects similar to the ones in the morning: cookies, chocolate, feathers, wild tobacco, tejuino, and flowers.

To begin the ceremony the participants were grouped in the following manner: On one ekipal was seated the marakame Huicho; next to him in the other ekipal was Vicente, occupying a place that to us seemed fundamental for the carrying out of the ceremony, since it was he who set the pattern for the songs sung by the marakame. Next to Vicente was placed a metal chair in which Pedro sat. Besides being second huichol singer, he had the task of playing a quite rudimentary small wooden violin. It was much smaller than a normal violin; nevertheless, its sound was strong enough not to be lost in a roofless enclosure. Next to Pedro, following the circle around the fire, was Tomás, the quiet Wirrarika who played a small guitar with characteristics similar to those of the little violin. Next to Tomás was the space set aside for the painting and the offerings placed next to it. The rest of the places were occupied indiscriminately and alternately by the different members of the group; even we occupied these places while attempting to integrate ourselves into the ritual, as the measure of our goodwill and ignorance of what steps to follow allowed us. Some of the members of the group remained standing.

All the Wirrarika of the group were reunited there. Women and children participated directly during the entire ritual. The smallest children, while not obligated to participate, took part almost in the same capacity as the adults. Babies participate in their mother's arms. It is significant to us that because the Wirrarika participate in their ceremonies practically from the time they are born, to participate in these events while still nursing must have an influence on their later life as children, young people, and adults.

It was about nine in the evening when Pedro began to sing, accompanied by his small violin and the little guitar of Tomás, instruments used exclusively in the rituals. Pedro intoned songs in Wirrarika for about twenty minutes, "to warm up," as he put it. The structure of the songs appeared to be melodic segments that varied after a time. Pedro's voice, his attitude, and his personality in general, changed completely the moment he began to sing. We were ignorant of what the texts were saying, but judging by the delivery of the singer, we supposed them to be of a very intense significance to the group. On another day we would comprehend the "why" of this delivery, when in reply to one of our questions, Pedro would tell us that those songs "had been taught to him by God" that very night.

Once Pedro finished singing, Huicho removed his small feathered staff from a small case made of palm leaves. This staff, the muvieri, he would hold in his right hand for the entire ceremony. At that moment there were placed at the feet of both singers two small pieces of red flannel upon which all through the night the various objects used in the ritual were deposited and sometimes withdrawn. The objects on this flannel were so precious that they were not to touch the ground, and they could only be handled by the singers during the Peyote ceremony. The ritual objects were similar to what was on the first altar, as well as the sacred tobacco, gourds containing sacred water, power objects of the singer, candles, and many buttons of the precious cactus. At this point the group of Wirrarika began to speak in their language. It was as if from this moment, the only language that could be spoken was Wirrarika, and the only world that had significance was the magic world that, through their myths, the Wirrarika were able to incarnate. After conversing for a while, the Wirrarika became silent.

Huicho, the huichol singer, raised his muvieri and began to sing. Everyone became very attentive. The song of the marakame was not accompanied by the musical instruments; rather he sang by himself, a cappella. The music coming from his lips was different from any other music we had heard. The words were pronounced with an accent distinct from that which they use normally; it even seemed to us that probably these songs were sung in some sacred language reserved for special occasions such as the one we were attending. The songs of Huicho were, in general, short metric segments repeated with melodic variations to the end. He repeated the same musical idea for a period of about forty minutes, and then changed it for another.

The marakame had been singing for about twenty minutes when something happened that surprised us: Pedro began to tune his violin and Tomás his little guitar. They plucked them softly to verify their intonation. This was happening while the marakame was singing so it gave the impression of breaking the air of solemnity and respect. Our surprise increased when Pedro, accompanied by the violin and the guitar, started singing, at the same time, a different melody from what Huicho was singing. At the beginning, we did not understand what was happening, but as they continued singing, we realized that these two melodies that had seemed so different in the beginning harmonized themselves to form a more complex melodic phenomenon. Listening to the techniques they employed, we began to think the Wirrarika were familiar with the technique of counterpoint long before Europe would know it through baroque music. Huicho and Pedro sang "counterpoint" for more or less half an hour after which there was silence for four or five minutes.

Next Huicho introduced a new series of songs with a distinct melodic structure, only on this occasion, after he had sung what seemed like a complete stanza, the rest of the Wirrarika answered him in chorus, repeating the same melody, after which followed a new one by the marakame and again a repetition by the group. The songs went on in this way for maybe forty or fifty minutes.

Then Pedro began to play and sing similar to the way he had done before, only now there was added a new element. At the moment Pedro began to sing and play the violin, the Wirrarika started a dance that—interrupted only at intervals—would last all night. The dance of the Wirrarika consisted of a rhythmic movement in which the feet were the most active, trying to follow the sounds produced by the violin. The hands remained quiet, hanging at their sides, or inside the pockets of their sweater if they had one. The body was kept leaning slightly to the front and in addition to the continuous stamping of the feet, there were movements toward the front, back, and to the sides. During the ceremony there were presented three basic elements, which were carried out alternately or combined indiscriminately: the song of the marakame, the music of the violin and guitar, accompanied by Pedro's singing, and the dancing of the Wirrarika. There were moments when the marakame sang alone; others in which

two distinct melodies were sung at the same time by adding
Pedro's melody to that of Huicho; and others in which the
people danced accompanied only by Pedro's songs as well as
the violin and guitar.

The cold increased gradually. At one o'clock in the morning it reached its maximum, close to 32 degrees F., and stayed
there until morning. Without cringing from the cold, the
Wirrarika continued with their ceremony as though nothing
had occurred. The marakame, who wore only a light shirt,
covered his back with a mantle. Vicente wrapped himself in a
blanket, but he did not fail to answer Huicho's songs the
entire night. We could not get over feeling impressed by the
resistance of these people who, with or without the cold,
endured entire nights without sleeping as though it were
nothing, since they—according to our information—had ceremonies lasting several days with their respective nights. We
were especially amazed how the marakame, a man of
advanced age, could withstand close to fifteen hours singing
in the bitter cold, which only subsided with the rising of the
sun. The entire night passed amid songs and dances, interrupted only momentarily, to be continued shortly thereafter.

From the beginning of the ceremony, Pedro from time to
time distributed pieces of peyote to each one of the participants with the help of his brother Hilario. We noticed they
treated the cactus with care and reverence. Before giving a
piece of Hikuri (peyote) to someone, he had to place it on the
eyes, ears, heart, and throat of the person receiving it "in order
to see, in order to hear, in order to feel, in order to be able to
sing." It was very clear to us that peyote is a fundamental element in the cosmovision of the Wirrarika. They use it not only
to see, to speak, and hear their gods, but also to cure illness
and tiredness, and to ensure good harvests. It is present, in
some form, in the majority of their activities.

We were eager, curious, to know the effect the cactus
would have on these people so far removed from our world
where psychotropic plants are used not only in an irreverent

manner but in a degrading one as well. Everyone took the Hikuri, men and women alike. The older children took it also, although in lesser quantities than the adults. It should be mentioned that none of the Wirrarika lost control or displayed behavior that could be termed inappropriate. What we did observe was a very intense emotion in each one of the participants, which we attributed more to the sacredness of the ceremony than to the effects of the peyote.

The ceremony was not in any way monotonous and the emotive response of the participants was highly variable. At a certain moment the song of the marakame became more serious, more sensitive; his voice began in midrange and finished in a clear falsetto that gave the melody a very sweet flavor. His muvieri vibrated as though it was driven by the power of his throat or by some ineffable force. His face displayed such strong emotion that we were profoundly impressed. Tears ran down his cheeks and at times his voice seemed to break. From time to time he wiped the tears from his face with the sleeve of his old shirt. The majority of the Wirrarika were weeping, even the older children. To see these men and women, generally so joyful, crying in that way, produced a lump in the throat and caused us to ask: What is it these people are seeing? What is the nature of their visions? What are their gods telling them?

We felt admiration and respect for these people who have been able to preserve their identity, resisting not only the passage of time, but also—and this was the most admirable—the pressure of the "civilized" world during five centuries of infamy. Neither the weapons of colonialism, nor the "goodwill" of the missionaries, could despoil for them the magical inheritance of their ancestors. This people, who possess nothing, and whose lands have been taken away, along with the possibility of cultivating the few remaining pieces, continue in spite of it all, defending their world, their language, and their traditions as though to shout at the history and the vanity of the whites: We are still here!

When it seemed the sadness had reached intolerable limits, the violin of Pedro and the guitar of Tomás came to rescue the participants from the melancholy that had taken hold of them. The dance seemed to animate them and the voice of Pedro was very reassuring. Some smiles appeared on the teary faces; the feeling of brotherhood was evident from the silent, but very expressive faces. When, in what seemed a most inopportune moment but in reality was the most appropriate, Cirilo told a joke, we observed the great ease with which the Wirrarika passed, in one moment, from one state of being to its opposite.

In those few moments when songs as well as dances were interrupted, the Wirrarika conversed among themselves or with Grandfather Fire. During the entire ceremony there was always someone to care for the feeding of Tatewari. It was about 4:30 in the morning; the atmosphere around the fire had changed in such a way as to make it seem as though the day before and its everyday surroundings had been left far behind. Now the Wirrarika spoke in a low voice, they displayed an attitude of reciprocal camaraderie very intimate and much more profound than when we had seen them during the day. We were sharing the mystery of being alive; we were travelers in pursuit of the Spirit, which also implied the difficult experience of "looking at our lives."

The marakame began to sing again; his voice, somewhat spent from the hours of effort, nevertheless displayed a spiritual intensity it had not had at the beginning. He was relating with his song the history of the world, and the messages given them by the Great-Grandfather Tail of the Deer: Tamatz Kahullumary.

Toward morning the marakame Huicho seemed to reach the point of maximum effort, not so much in relation to the entire night's work as that one of the most important aspects of the work of the singer is to help the sun to defeat the stars so he can come out. The song of the marakame is company and a stimulus for the Sun. The Wirrarika believe that every night, in some place in their territory, there is at least one marakame tending to the responsibility of helping the Sun (that night the responsibility was Huicho's). Thus it happened that at the moment when the first rays of the Sun began to appear, the Wirrarika became euphoric and joyful. The Sun had heard their songs! They had participated in the solar miracle! With the dawn, new elements were added to the ritual. The marakame stood up and received the rays of the Sun without ceasing to sing, pointed his muvieri, which is also considered an arrow, toward the Sun. The light of day seemed to infuse him with new life, the exhaustion that a short while before had begun to appear in his face disappeared. All of their faces seemed transformed, giving the impression of their feeling sacred after having incarnated their myths. The marakame took a long rope, which he had prepared. Everyone stood up and grouped together around the fire, which continued to crackle. Huicho began to pass the rope around the group. Each one took the rope with his hands behind his back and passed it to the next. The rope went around twice. The singing of the marakame was continuous. As Pedro himself told us: "Now all of us are one." The rope was withdrawn.

The next step was the sacrifice. Vicente and Hilario brought a goat that had been tied up in another part of the patio. The animal bleated as though it had a presentiment of the destiny in store for it. While the marakame continued to sing standing and pointing his magic feathers at the Sun, Vicente and Hilario laid the animal down in front of the painting of yarn figures. Vicente took out his knife and sank it into the breast of the goat, immediately placing a small container next to the bleeding wound to collect the precious liquid. Pedro took the container and, with a feather, sprinkled drops of blood on each one of the participants as well as on the majority of the ritual objects, principally the candles. The animal continued to emit its last bleatings while the women lit candles, which they passed to everyone. The singer with his song and the power of his feathers directed the goat's soul on the way to its destiny: the Sun. The peyote was still periodically distributed. When the animal was dead, the marakame took a small cup of water from a sacred site. With a white flower previously wetted in the cup, he sprinkled a few drops of sacred water on the lips and then on the head of each one of the participants. Upon doing this, he uttered a few words. Once everyone had been touched with the magic water, each took a button of Hikuri, cutting it into small pieces and then distributing it to all the rest. Everyone exchanged a piece of the sacred cactus, first having placed it on the heart, eyes, and ears of the person who was going to eat it. When everyone had finished distributing the peyote, the marakame stopped singing.

It was about 10:30 in the morning. More than fourteen hours had passed since the ceremony began. The last step was changing the names of the participants. The procedure was as follows: They placed a pot of water between the fire and the marakame, who had sat down again. The people took turns one by one. They leaned over the pot of water. They removed a little and washed their face and hands. They got up. At that moment Pedro and Huicho began, in their tongue and in a humorous tone, to discuss the person who had washed his or her face, and they then gave each a new name. Each time someone was "baptized," the rest laughed at the new name. When Pedro's turn came, it was Huicho who "baptized" him. Finally, Pedro chose a name for Huicho who would not escape the "baptism" just because he was a marakame. As far as we could tell, with that the ceremony was finished.

What followed was a little more lively, having to do with cutting up and cooking the goat, the meal for that day. Curiously the marakame designated two of us to skin it. The choice took us by surprise, but Guadalupe offered to lend us a hand in the task of skinning the goat, for which he had more experience than we.

The ceremony had ended and the world began, little by

little, to be once more the everyday world for the Wirrarika as well as for us. Although we had only taken part in it as "observer-participants," we were very grateful to the group of Wirrarika who offered us the opportunity to be together with them in an experience that allowed us a glimpse, however slight, into their magic world.

EIGHT
OMEN
ON THE
SACRED
MOUNTAIN

(In the following narration I have deliberately omitted details of the specific form of some of the exercises and rituals. By their nature they are not easy to carry out lacking the appropriate conditions, particularly without the help of a person well versed in such procedures. Trying to do them without such help would not be of any advantage anyway.)

Ten years had passed since my first encounter with the Wirrarika. It was more than thirteen years since my incursions into the country with indigenous peoples of different ethnic groups, and eleven since I had begun to coordinate human development groups with different lines of work.

It was the first time I had made the delicate decision to take a work group to the sacred land of the Indians. Before, I had shared some experiences in indigenous territory with one or two of my companions in the struggle, outside the context of groups and courses.

I had taken the most highly developed groups on hikes in the mountains, even approaching the periphery of communities that preserved some of the more unusual practices having to do with alternate forms of awareness.[1] I have always considered direct contact with the living races of Toltequity something that should be dealt with very carefully. It was apparent to me that it would be a mistake to bring my friends, or advanced participants of my groups, to an encounter with the Indian world without a very clear sign indicating it should be done. It didn't matter if the sign was very late in coming or if it never came at all. At any rate, the indigenous element was rather a basic nutrient of my work with groups, not a point of destination.

I also held the conviction that, before contact with other ways of life and perception—which can only with difficulty be made use of from the perspective of our ordinary description of the modern world with its aims and interest—it was necessary for participants to put their daily affairs in order. The surmounting of basic ties and limits of personal history, the training and disciplined use of the attention, the disregard for mental and emotional obsessions, the overcoming of addictions of all types, the general cleansing of the physical and energetic body, the recovery of sensitivity, and the capacity to stop the internal dialogue, are necessary for the person to be able to handle the everyday world with efficiency and an internally balanced orientation. Under those conditions, an encounter with alternative realities could contribute to the development of the individual.

Attempts to access states of nonordinary reality without a

---

[1] It should be mentioned that such adventures were carried out very infrequently since I wasn't working with several groups at once. Rather I started—at most—one group per year and did not begin another until I had finished my "formal" work with the preceding one.

minimum of order and a necessary strengthening of the *tonal*[2] were generally futile. If by chance they were achieved without the necessary groundwork of a strong and balanced life, the results tended to be dangerous. Likewise, the indigenous experience for a person lacking adequate progress on the way of the warrior, became a tourist-type excursion for Indian "folklore," or even, when carried out that way, a foray into areas that were intensely dangerous.

Many men and women who had worked with me had achieved significant advances in the search for a true life and in areas such as those mentioned on an individual basis. We had not yet attained comparable change by a complete generation—that is, by a work group in which all its members had achieved such a level of development. Many individuals during the course of our experience had attained discipline and control of themselves and of their daily lives, and they were the ones most competent for encounters of this nature. But, there were very few who had the spiritual inclination and the degree of availability for a battle like that. In general those were persons who had achieved levels of fulfillment and projects to which they were completely dedicated. On the other hand, the many who insistently manifested their interest in direct contact with the indigenous experience were by and large in very bad energetic and life conditions, and their interest in the indigenous was very similar to their interest in alternate realities: a mental experience by which they attempted to escape from themselves. Fortunately, the *otherness* of the indigenous world is closed to all those who do not meet the necessary requirements. This continues to be true even if an inept individual is physically in the middle of the most profound of rituals. To perceive that world, it is necessary to have "special eyes," which are found in every human being, but

---

[2] See the introduction and first chapter of *The Teachings of Don Carlos*, Bear & Company, Santa Fe, 1995.

they only open after a true struggle in pursuit of a true life, a strong life.

Consequently, I very rarely took people from the outside with me on my encounters in the Indian world, although in my inner conscience I secretly desired that others from the world of my origin could experience them with me. I wanted someone to talk to and share things about those worlds so strange and marvelous! In spite of my fantasies and personal nostalgia, I had long before realized that those who venture beyond the limits of everyday life have as companions solitude and the awareness of death. They witness and experience wonders to which they almost always arrive alone. This, for example, is what real mountain climbers know, those who go in pursuit of the highest peaks—on that side of reality there are very few people. Although—thinking about it—on the side of normality there are fewer. As Genaro said when he wanted to return to Ixtlan:[3] There are only phantoms! What is true is that beyond the cage known as the everyday world, there are far fewer people, but the few encountered there are much more real.

Getting back to our story, what I did was to institute an intermediate level of approach to the universe of the surviving Toltecs. That was the reason for the hikes and exercises carried out in the Sierra de Puebla and in different zones in the mountains of Oaxaca. These areas are saturated with centuries of the comings and goings of indigenous peoples. At the same time, those same sites and territories, those mountains and gorges, had physically and spiritually nourished the ancient Toltecs and their survivors today. Therefore—I reasoned—if we do sufficient work, without doubt we will be able to learn much in those places; and only if there were some very powerful sign would we leave the mountains and enter into contact with the communities themselves. The rule

---

[3] See *Journey to Ixtlan*, Carlos Castaneda, Penguin Books Ltd, Harmondsworth, Middlesex, England, 1973, p. 245.

we followed was not to disturb or trouble with our presence those communities close to which we would pass, and which were quite closed to outsiders, resigning ourselves to an encounter with the surrounding wilderness. Such experiences, by the way, turned out to be highly substantial, since they allowed us to know much about the world and about ourselves. Many fundamental techniques, in particular those favoring the connection with the awareness of the Earth, were developed there.

Within this scheme of "intermediate approach" to indigenous areas for groups with a good degree of development was a project that had never been carried out—to traverse the sacred desert of the survivors par excellence of ancient Toltequity: the Wirrarika. This was the place that had the highest value for me since its force was extraordinarily intense, signifying a Promise of Power and Knowledge, but also a danger.

I knew that to try to penetrate it without being sufficiently compact, energetically speaking, on an individual as well as group level, would be a suicidal task. Again the risks were of two types having to do with inadequate preparation: to not see anything beyond our own mental projections, or to confront highly dangerous physical risks. The least threatening was without doubt the abundance of rattlesnakes and scorpions. It was evident that a lack of clear purpose could turn into any type of problem along the way. This carried a very delicate responsibility.

For three years, we had made four attempts to penetrate the area under adequate conditions. The first three proved fruitless. The strategy we followed was: Once we had decided to try to enter the desert, we began preparations for the trip in the most conscientious manner possible, and we went ahead as long as there was no sign or manifestation to hold us back. We summed it up with the simple affirmation, "If the door opens, then we go through; if not, then we return." And that is how it was. The first three attempts were aborted almost as we were about to enter. The door remained closed because of a small argument between two group members, damage to one of the vehicles, lack of integration and coordination of the group as a whole, a storm, some incident with the people of the surrounding towns.

Anyone might think that such signs were too trivial and we could have gone on. For me there is no doubt we did the correct thing. Beyond external manifestations, the internal voice of Silent Knowledge hidden very deep within our being, which we can hear if we learn to employ the kind of attention necessary, told me what to do. At no time was I spurred on by anxiety, nor did I retreat out of fear. Given that our intent was not obsessive, rather almost indifferent, we returned on each occasion content and without the least feeling of frustration for not having been able to enter that sacred territory. Although I personally had the dream of someday being able to take a work group to those places, in reality it did not matter at all if one day it happened or not. In the end, the work was always to meet the challenges presented to us every day of our lives, and these tentative plans in the areas of "intermediate approach" did not form part of our general program. Therefore, having established that the door would not open, we returned to our previously scheduled experiences that, on the other hand, were very attractive and demanding.

But it did happen, however, that one fine day the door opened, and we went through.

Finally the requirements seemed to be met. The group had been working together for more than a year and we had achieved a compact group of participants who had met, step by step, the demands of the various workshops during the past thirteen months. Each person deserved to be there. They each had been certified with their effort and achievements in bettering the energetic quality of their lives and persons. My evaluation was that with the discipline and detachment they had achieved, they would be in condition to perform appropriately in the desert. Fortunately, beyond my personal considerations, there was a response from the place to our intention of entering it as group: Go ahead.

It happened in the following way:

For several months, I had talked to the group about taking a trip and carrying out various exercises relative to their stage of work. We would go to the desert zone of Central Mexico, which constitutes part of the sacred territory of the Wirrarika, who called it Humun' Kulluaby. The trip we would take would be in fact a ritual Pilgrimage to a sacred site where an immense power was concentrated. This ritual Pilgrimage would not be an idle imitation of rituals alien to our life experience; on the contrary, it would be a concrete and symbolic expression of the work that for some time we had been carrying out in the transformation of our lives.

Humun' Kulluaby has two meanings. On one hand, it denotes the entire region collectively, which includes a great expanse of desert and several mountains of which the tallest and most significant is called La' Unarre, also known as the "Palace of the Governor." At the same time, Humun' Kulluaby designates a very specific site within the plain of that great desert, precisely the destination of a Pilgrimage undertaken year after year by the Wirrarika belonging to the closed group of *peyoteros*. There they carry out the hunt for Deer-Peyote and its related rituals. Also, on occasion and for various reasons, Indians go to the place alone or accompanied exclusively by their family.

In agreement with the strategy of intermediate approach, our intention was to traverse the great desert, always keeping enough distance from the specific sites where the Wirrarika carried out their Pilgrimage so as not to interfere with or defile their sacred spaces.

The work plan we conceived included some similarities to the practices I had known during my experiences with the Wirrarika, particularly their way of approaching the world of nature, which for them is a sacred world and therefore magical. The walks of attention were a basic activity. Due to

Wirrarika influence, we would carry out that profound energetic arrangement they call "confession" and several ritual techniques related to the Grandfather Fire Tatewari. Also on the program were advanced techniques concerning separation from personal history and its fetishes. Having as an aid the powerful force of the place, we would have to be capable of linking ourselves to it by means of the special handling of attention.

It was clear beforehand that our objective was not the consumption of peyote or any other psychoactive plant we found there. In fact, among the minimum basic requirements the group members had to meet were overcoming such habits as tobacco, marijuana, alcohol, and other addictions. Some of them had waged arduous battles against some of these vices so for them it was inappropriate to approach "power plants." Although we would not physically consume the power plants that abound in the area, we realized that upon entering their habitat, we made ourselves accessible to their power. We were able to prove this later upon establishing that the force channeled through the Hikuri (peyote) affected our perception, our awareness, and our potentiality, placing us clearly in states of nonordinary reality without need of ingesting or even touching the sacred cactus, because all the place was full of its energetic power.

Besides the physical preparations for the experience, each one of the participants had undergone an internal preparation, which included learning to live in a tight, disciplined, and strong way. They had made an Offering to Power some time before that had to do with the realization of acts or changes in their daily life favorable to it and to the unification with the Spirit. Our norm was that any kind of ritual would produce empty results if it had no direct relation with the warrior's battle that we wage in the everyday world, in which the enemy to vanquish is ourselves and our limitations. As a symbolic expression of the battle, each one personally fabricated an offering or gift for the Powers that dwell there, which would be delivered at the appropriate time and place.

With the preparations completed and topographical maps of the area studied, we were on our way. My work plan was, naturally, an "open" one that would have to adjust itself to the demands of the place and the development of events. In fact, the initial trek was a journey without a firm destination decided on beforehand, which would terminate with the selection of some appropriate campsite to carry out our work.

We traveled the highway without problems. The fears and natural apprehension about what was in store for us were eased by the atmosphere of camaraderie and good humor prevailing among "the pilgrims."

We arrived at the dusty hamlet that constituted the village of San . . . located on the edge of the desert. After finding an appropriate spot, we made ready to begin the hike. It was about one o'clock and the sun burned hot over the desert. On the horizon, as far as the eye could see, was the desert of San Luis Potosi with its characteristic chaparral and cacti. Toward the left in the distance was the range of the Sacred Mountain. We did not have a specific direction to go, but in some way I knew that La' Unarre would be our beacon. If I remained attentive to its presence, I would encounter the appropriate route. We lined up in the traditional "Indian file" and quickly began to walk, seeking to enter the desert and approach the mountains.

First we began to take paths that "supposedly" opened between the bushes. I say supposedly because as we advanced they branched off, crossed others, and disappeared only to appear later. Finally we accepted the fact that in the desert there are no paths other than those we make as we walk. Each direction offered a possible way. The sun increased its intensity and I was glad I had not forgotten my straw hat or my bandanna. I found myself at the head of the line without a specific destination; we were going nowhere, but nevertheless I felt happy.

Walking toward the mysterious is something I have always liked. To move on and on confident that if the purpose is indeed clear to the heart—although it will not be to the mind—I will arrive at the place I seek, although I do not know which place that may be. Breathing in rhythm, eyes alert, face relaxed. Sure and rhythmic stride, always focusing on where or on what I was stepping. The minutes passed and I discovered the murmur of the desert. That sound, so characteristic that it cannot be explained in any way other than the vibration of the place, is properly called the sound of silence. As time passed, that vibration was not only heard but was felt throughout the entire body. It was as though all the atmosphere was tense or formed a magnetic field inside which I had to move with a great deal of attention.

Walking in the desert, we discovered that as our legs worked more and more, we did not become weary; to the contrary, the hike toned us up and harmonized us with the surroundings, which made us feel better and better. As the hours passed, that undefined word "desert," which upon our arrival had become the landscape, was transformed into an unfolding world, gradually revealing itself. Entering the desert is not only entering its geographical area and walking around; it really means to open our senses and our heart to become permeated by it. It is then that the world and the landscape transform themselves into what always has been far from us, waiting for us to venture forth sufficiently. And when we find out that the desert is a separate world, that which supposedly should be empty becomes filled to the brim. Overflowing with sound, overflowing with life, overflowing with energy and beauty. The desert, with its vegetation, with its horizon, with its silence, its equilibrium, its sunsets and its clean air, is the opportunity to enter into a world where one is closer to the Spirit. Not only the Spirit that animates and sustains the world, but also its presence inside us.

At a certain moment now well into the afternoon, I singled out a place to camp relatively close to the mountains. We moved toward the indicated spot. As we entered, we felt a kind of freshness that differentiated it from other places through which we passed. The place seemed hospitable and secure from the first moment. The freshness of the atmosphere, the blue-grayish tonalities of the sunset, and the feeling of the place, immediately told us the selection was correct. About sixty meters from where we were, we made out the edge of . . . a river? Yes, it looked like the bed of a river, naturally without water. I asked myself if at some time during the year it carries water . . . a river in the desert? In any case, I calculated the sand in the dry bed would be satisfactory to spend the night on. We went over there and there was another surprise: the place was full of peyote. We came closer and observed that underneath the small bushes were complete families of the sacred cactus. Some were by themselves while others were in pairs or groups of up to fifteen. Certain ones had a beautiful flower on top.

Without a doubt the place we selected is none other than the home of Hikuri, the powerful Spirit who dwells in the peyote plant and according to the Wirrarika is one of the manifestations of the Blue Deer, Tamatz Kahullumary! For a moment I wondered if it would be too risky to camp there, but the feeling this place gave us was beneficent and friendly. The Power of the place was felt in every pore of the body. I told myself: We're already here and as for Power, we were here only with Power. Thus I reaffirmed my conviction that to act with carelessness or weakness in a place of Power would be inappropriate, and even dangerous.

After I cautioned everyone to abstain from touching the Hikuri, we crossed with care the field of peyote until we arrived at the dry riverbed. Although it was completely dry, I realized it was alive, since the Spirit of the water was felt clearly. I knew this was a good campsite and if we were in danger, returning to this place alone would be protection enough.

We set to gathering dry branches, or anything that looked

like firewood for the home of Tatewari. We collected "the wood" with extreme care, thus achieving a double purpose— we avoided careless contact with any poisonous animal or with the abundant thorns, and we continued to cultivate our attention to allow states of heightened awareness. Once we had enough "wood," we erected the tents, then ate our first food of the day, although some continued to fast.

Everything passed in a peculiar atmosphere. Without any intervening instruction on my part, everyone's attitude was attentive and silent, no one wanted to disturb the peace and equilibrium of the desert. Each one was mindful of particular tasks, without superfluous talk or the dispersion of attention. Night began to fall. I felt content upon realizing that finally, after so many years, I have been able to bring a compact and well-prepared group to a place like this. What new paths will open themselves to us once the door has been opened?

We walked to a small clearing to await the darkness. Nobody said anything, some remained standing while others lay down on the ground. In the twilight we remained immobile and silent; we harmonized with the rocks and the bushes, with the shadows of the night that began to arise. Feeling and accepting the vibration of the desert, harmonizing and submerging ourselves in its frequency. Just that. Nothing else. If there is no movement, no sound, if we do nothing other than just "be there," we become one with the desert, with the sunset. Our everyday noisy self disappeared with all its history amidst that tranquillity and absolute peace.

The world turned completely dark and our pupils dilated. The darkness was illusory. In reality we could see in the dark. A kind of dark blue light permitted us to distinguish a world of forms and shapes. There was no need for flashlights. After all, we ourselves were also shadows. The temperature was very agreeable, not hot, not cold, cool. The clock said several hours had passed; for us time stood still. I deemed the time had arrived to pass to other activities and I saw that all the

The Wirrarika home.

To travel into this mountain is to travel into oneself.

The ceremonial center in Santa Isabel.

The Kalihuey is the gathering center of the jicareros and Tatewari, the Grandfather Fire.

Getting into Tatei Matinieri.

Deep emotions when the pilgrims present their offerings to
Tatei Matinieri.

We bring offerings for the Sacred Place.

My eagle-feathered muvieri has found its
first hikuri.

Tatei Matinieri is the eyes of our Mother the Earth.

A pathway from the desert to La' Unarre, the highest place on Humun' Kulluaby.

Pilgrims getting to the top of La' Unarre, the Sacred Mountain, also known as the "Palace of the Governor."

"We have arrived!" say the bullhorns to the Poderios.

We came here to open our hearts and see our life.

Offerings to La' Unarre.

Tatei Neirra, the drum ceremony.

Teokaris (partners of the Sacred Path).

members of the group were integrated into a single body we call a *muegano*.[4] No one realized when it happened. In any event, without agreeing to and without awareness on anyone's part, they had grouped together into a muegano. I looked at the sky and I again remembered that always when I believed I have already witnessed all the beauty possible, the world shows us there is more, always more, until the moment of our death. The sky was so full of stars that the band of the Milky Way could be distinguished clearly. Thanking life from our hearts for having given us the miracle of living, of realizing it and being able to verify it in a place such as this, we made ready for subsequent activities.

First was the lighting of the fire. We did it carefully, following each one of the steps I had learned among my Indian brothers of the mountains. The ritual lighting of the fire, with all its details, opens the door to entering a true relationship with the great-great-grandfather, the most ancient of all the powers, the Fire Tatewari. The night in the desert passed amid silent observation of the fire, songs of Power, and some dances. Some went to sleep a little before dawn. Others remained speaking with the great-grandfather, to ask advice or help, to thank him for his heat and light, his *nierika*.[5] No one wanted to enter the tents when they were so content outside.

The Powers of the place allowed themselves to be felt with

---

[4] Muegano is the name for a type of Mexican candy that always appears in whimsical forms. In this case the word refers to a pleasant gathering of people lying on or reclining one on top of another without order or harmony, and used to alleviate the cold, to rest, or simply for the pleasure of physical closeness.

[5] Nierika is a word with many meanings. Depending on the context it can mean view, vision (what is obtained during a ritual), mirror (the one used by the marakame in order to determine the designs of grandfather fire), or offering (a yarn painting done over a wooden base upon which they shape the visions they have had during the ritual, in which case it constitutes an offering).

intensity. The Spirit of Hikuri was there, active, pushing us toward the world of the mirrors where we can view our life and our heart with its luminous parts as well as its withered parts.

The next day we carried out different exercises of the first and second attention. We examined the surrounding desert to be able to return later to "our place." The exercises we performed became more effective due to the energetic intensity found there. Our perception increased and the motivation of our hearts was greater than the force of our attachments. We could see and comprehend. All this prepared us for the decisive battle that would be waged that night. In accordance with the energetic characteristics and the background of each one of the group members, I made the decision to form two independent parties of warriors for the task that evening. Those who have led more uncontrolled and conflictive lives made up the right hemisphere of our group; those who have had more balanced lives composed the left hemisphere. Each party had its own encampment and its own fire, about three hundred meters distant from each other.

In the first part of the exercises, which would begin a few hours before twilight and last to the end of the day, the two hemispheres would work together in one of the most powerful exercises carried out so far. It dealt with an arduous hand-to-hand battle against the fetishes of the personal ego. Given the force of the enemy, we could not be sure of victory beforehand. Later, each one of the groups would undertake a program of distinct activities. The left hemisphere would work with techniques and rituals giving access to the separate reality, the awareness of the other self, while the right hemisphere would work with techniques guiding to the discovery and development of nonordinary ways of handling everyday reality. Together they would represent and would experience the two areas of the warrior's task, which are in fact, the two areas of the world and of the person: *tonal* and *nagual*.

Toward afternoon, the battle against the fetish of the

personal ego was at its apogee. Each one of the group members had gone alone into the desert, and the din of battle could be heard from where I was in the dry riverbed. It was impressive! I really doubted if anyone would come out victorious. I was mostly confident they would come back all right; at times though I wondered if I would see return those monstrous ego fetishes now fortified by their victory over life. The image of that horde of fetishes returning to camp gave me the shivers. Finally they began to return one by one. They were my friends, their faces reflecting the deep feeling of a battle that had touched very profound fibers within their being. They were no longer carrying the fetishes, but it was not time yet for euphoria. Night had hardly fallen and there were still many things to do.

After each group had instructions, we said good-bye to those who would work the techniques for the right side. The farewell was emotional and we all wished our counterparts great success in their struggle. We were aware that in this particular case, the positive results obtained by one group were necessary for the success of the other. I went to work with those who would adventure into the left side of awareness.

We chose our site about three hundred meters or more from the other group, which remained in the dry riverbed. We made sure we could not see or hear our companions on the right side, not even shouting. We performed the ritual of lighting the fire and got set up. As in all such exercises, everything begins with the observation of the fire and the silencing of thoughts. Then followed the exercises to summon the powers present there. We opened ourselves to them to awaken the awareness of the other self, the awareness of the *nagual*.

There were ritual movements and songs that helped us to cross the threshold between the two sides of awareness. Of what we saw and what happened there, I cannot say much, since the visions and experiences of each one were very personal, although we kept our awareness linked together at all times. For me in particular it was a decisive night. Three substantial questions had been needling me for a long time about which direction I should follow in my personal life, in the areas of my work with the groups and with the Indians. Answers came to me then. Each question and each answer constituted a battle, at times painful. When at last the answer was clear in my inner being, I felt inclined to tell it to my good friend René, asking him to please help me remember it, that what I had found was too important to allow myself to forget it when I returned to right-side awareness. Toward the end of the third answer, which dealt with the equilibrium between my emotional relationships and the demands of my task, the nostalgia that produces the direct perception of the mysterious and the solitude it implies came to a very intense point.

I turned toward La' Unarre, my companions turned to look as well, some pointing with their fingers and with an expression of amazement. The Sacred Mountain was shining! From its summit emerged enormous rays of light, like an immense reflector! Rafael began to walk and told everyone: "We have to go there, it's calling us!" For a moment everyone pondered. The feeling of the call was clear, but to start out from a point so far away in the middle of the night? By day it would take at least five hours to arrive at the base of the mountain and who knows how many to climb from the desert to the summit?

I told everyone that we would take on the challenge to respond to that call later, and that, for now, the battle was here, on the spot where we were. Nevertheless, everyone felt the need to take a hike in the darkness, which meant leaving our selected sites. The Wirrarika say that in Humun' Kulluaby there dwell not only the Blue Deer and the rest of the powers of the desert, but also the Kakayares, which can appear as devils of many kinds. In accordance with our nonindigenous upbringing, we didn't believe in gods and demons, but through experience we knew that the world was inhabited by all kinds of things, entities or energies, which could be perceived with much more facility in places like this one. If we perceived them, what mattered least was the name given them, and though reason told us there was nothing to fear, our bodies remained very much on the alert. The hike lasted about an hour during which there certainly were manifested all sorts of strange things, but we stayed together and, with controlled attention, we were able to face those exciting moments with sobriety. The Palace of the Governor remained shining until after we returned from the hike.

At about five in the morning, after many hours in left-side awareness, we fell asleep.

About eight in the morning we awoke very content to see that we were all there. Each one had received very valuable lessons relative to his or her search. We felt great desire to find the right-side group, to know how it had gone with them. We hastened to pack up our campsite and go meet them. The encounter was very joyous.

They had also had a very substantial night, giving as testimony a very beautiful and intense song they had composed, of which they sang a portion.

What followed was a very delicious breakfast that, together with the young morning sun, put us in very high spirits.

THE PALACE

The group maintained its rhythmic pace walking Indian file. We had just left the town of Real de Catorce, with its ruined houses and abandoned mines. The way to La' Unarre is through a succession of bald hills, although the majority possess a fine layer of grass, which gives them a mild green color. The air turned humid and cold as we ascended. From the height we could see an entire succession of hills with the desert in the distance. There were no trees, no houses, no people. Only a vagrant stray burro. And of course, the pilgrims. A feeling of joy inspired me when I realized that we were walking on paths used for centuries or millennia by travelers searching for the Spirit, over this same earth, in this same scenery, and under this same sky. Also it gave me joy to know

that we were not so far from those travelers, since our climb
was not for idle fun or for sport. Rather it was part of a way of
life and a search chosen by me many years ago. We also
walked toward the Spirit. We also searched for our Blue Deer.

There are many things I did not understand, but which I
could clearly feel. We were in sacred territory. From the stories
I had heard about the wonders that occur here, according to
Wirrarika cosmogony, I felt there was a fundamental significance concerning this mountain, which continued to elude
me. It was as though something were hidden here, under the
soil, behind every rock, ready to manifest itself if only we
knew the proper invocation.

We continued the ascent, which became steeper. At various points we found that the narrow path, at times invisible,
divided itself where two hills met. From there the summit of
the Palace was not visible, being hidden by the intervening
hills. I went to the head of the line and had to stay very alert
so as not to take the wrong route, for we could end up on the
summit of another mountain of similar height but very far
from our objective. The walk of attention continued. It felt
especially intense. I turned around and corroborated with
pleasure what my body had been clearly feeling—no one had
fallen behind and everyone was walking in the same rhythm
like a single being. These people have learned to walk correctly after all. The familiar sensation of forming part of a larger
energy body, to go as though encapsulated inside a kind of
energy vault containing the entire group was very clear. The
ego was asleep and the sensation of being only part of a much
larger body was comforting. Indeed. Any one of us was a
small part of the body of the group whose awareness was connected through the magic of attention. As Octavio Paz says:
"There is no you, there is no me, it is always us."[6] We also con-

---

[6] "Piedra de Sol" from *Libertad Bajo Palabra*, Octavio Paz, Fondo de
Cultura Economica, second edition, Mexico City, 1990.

nected ourselves with a much larger body, Tlaltipac (Earth), which in Wirrarika territory should be called Tatei Urianaka, and through her we connected in harmony with everything existing. With a mother like that, experiencing the world like that, we definitely could not be bored. There was no room for self-pity, or for vanity. There was only room to see, feel, and breathe. To move.

Finally the summit of the Palace could be clearly seen. We continued ahead, the sacredness of the place becoming more evident as we approached the sanctuary where Tamatz Kahullumary was born. The peculiar energy there became more and more intense, as though we were approaching a reactor that, however, was not menacing; rather it exuded a most exquisite peace. We were also changing. An internal awareness was imposing itself over the mental noise and limited vision of everyday life.

We traversed the last stretch separating us from the summit. The terrain was so steep that, in spite of having only about twenty meters to go, we could not see what lay on the other side. We arrived at the summit and saw, first thing, the diaphanous immensity of the desert. There below lay Humun' Kulluaby. The air was completely transparent, and the view was lost on the distant horizon. The tiny villages, which could be made out only with difficulty, did not in any way alter the natural scenery. As far as the eye could see, in all directions, only nature reigned, the Spirit. I looked at my companions and realized that we were all immersed in this experience to the very core of our being. Watery eyes expressed peace and joy, revealing the intimate feeling this journey had for each one. Definitely, to walk among these places had an effect on us.

The place was full of signs revealing the frequent presence of the Wirrarika people: the perfect circle where they give life to the Grandfather Fire, the offerings placed in many parts around the summit—arrows, nierikas, god's eyes, deer antlers, candles, chocolate, mirrors, and many other things. I gave instructions for everyone to refrain from moving or touching anything. Not even a rock.

The summit of the Palace has a slight cleft in the middle, which divides it into two well-differentiated zones. On the left side, where we found the offerings, is the area in which the Wirrarika carry out their rituals. We located ourselves in the right-hand area, about two hundred meters from the "Wirrarika zone." Once we had organized our things and lighted the fire, we prepared to deliver our offering to the Power of the Mountain. By this time, the delivery of the offering had attained a much more profound meaning than we could have imagined at the beginning. Each one proceeded in his or her own manner, selecting a place, and in solitude voicing feelings, expressing to the mountain the significance of the offering. This was the culmination of our task in this temple made by nature.

As it was already late, we decided to spend the night there. After gathering "firewood," we created a circle of rocks and made a big fire. With no specific task to do, we talked around the fire, discussing our lives, our struggle, and what repercussions this experience would have on our subsequent efforts. Without doubt we would never be the same after this double journey, the one outside and the one inside. During the night, the cold felt at this altitude was really intense. The wind was icy. In the darkness, the other face of the world was revealed in all its mystery and inexplicable sensations. We slept very little.

At dawn, the prospect of returning home loomed near. I got out of my sleeping bag and greeted the morning, the desert, and the Sacred Mountain. I was thankful for the new day. I began to plan, mentally, the itinerary for our return. My companions were still asleep, so I decided to walk around. Unconsciously I went toward the left side of the summit; then all of a sudden I felt an internal jolt, doubting whether what I was seeing was real, or a product of my imagination. A compact group of Indians was ascending and was about to arrive at the summit. This I certainly did not expect. So much walking about in these sites, cognizant of the Wirrarika footprints, feeling their presence, then when we are almost ready to depart, they make their appearance. The group consisted of nine members, all dressed in the attire typical of the Wirrarika: trousers of richly embroidered cloth, shirts of intense colors open at the sleeves, bandannas, hats with feathers, and handbags filled with everything necessary for the journey and the rituals. I observed once more their way of walking, which for years I have been studying. A resolute pace and rhythm. Absolute silence. Their faces imbued with a sacredness that revealed to me that the ascent of La' Unarre was only a part of the physical and spiritual journey that surely had lasted several days.

I remained quiet, in a squatting position. I observed carefully to see if there were any Wirrarika I knew among them. There did not appear to be. They must be from some other community than those I have visited in the mountains. I relaxed a little—as my companions were still asleep and some distance away, the Indians wouldn't be disturbed in their tasks. They passed close by me and we exchanged a gesture of greeting. It was clear they were at a high point in their Pilgrimage. This was not the time to talk and exchange courtesies. Feeling their presence so close, I realized I could see their bodies, but their awareness was very far away, in a world that continued to escape my perception. They moved with complete security, they acted in precise synchronization in everything they did without saying a single word. They passed by heading for the area of the offerings. Instinctively I turned around and saw one of my friends. He was one of the members of the group who had a more profound handling of attention and one of the few who had had previous experiences with the Wirrarika. I made a movement of my head to come closer. We observed that the Wirrarika were in a moment of intense activity. They were about sixty meters from us. They had formed a circle and were speaking in their tongue; but they were not conversing but performing a ritual. The marakame moved his muvieri and blessed each one of the pilgrims. Many other things occurred whose significance I did not understand.

I experienced a strange fascination and felt the need to be there inside the ceremony. We approached very cautiously to a distance of about ten meters from the Wirrarika, very alert for any possible sign of disapproval on their part, in which case we would withdraw immediately. The Wirrarika noticed our presence but did not react in any way. They continued with what they were doing. As the rituals continued, the level of energetic intensity increased. Those men were not seeing the same world as we were; they were seeing much further beyond. I felt absurd, observing something that "pulled" me intensely but that I could not understand. At times I felt like an intruder, but the fascination that these people and their practices exerted on me had me glued to the spot. In spite of the fact that I have known Wirrarika for years, that I have lived with them in their communities and had marvelous experiences that have made me feel very close to them, there exist large areas of their rituals that continue to be incomprehensible to me. Moments of interaction in which I have not been able to enter. There, in front of me, was one of those moments.

I had never been invited—and I had never asked to go— on the most significant spiritual journey of the Wirrarika: the Pilgrimage to Humun' Kulluaby. Certainly I was familiar with the places and passed through them with my Wirrarika friends, but never as part of a true Pilgrimage. It was not that I had not gone on a Pilgrimage with them that made me feel one step apart from them, but basically because the world into which they entered during their most significant rituals continued to elude me. Therefore I had never wanted to force events in order to "sneak into" a Pilgrimage. Besides, I was well aware that I was not Wirrarika. I had made ritual Pilgrimages on several occasions that had brought me truly to the Spirit. Nevertheless, the way in which these direct inheritors of the ancient Toltec traditions embarked on journeys through awareness was a phenomenon that could do little more than fascinate me.

Seeing these human beings singing to the Earth, to the mountains, and to the Powers of the world, I felt like a privileged observer looking through the screen of a time tunnel. There those men were, taking the same steps and carrying out the same rituals as had their ancestors more than a thousand years ago. Without any reference (our presence notwithstanding) to the direction that peoples of modern societies had taken. The same scene could very well have occurred exactly the same way fifty, one hundred, two hundred, or one thousand years ago. We have so much to learn from these men and women who insist on regarding the Sun, the clouds, the mountains, and every other naturally occurring manifestation, as the visible face of the Spirit and therefore sacred!

Looking at the Wirrarika on their Sacred Summit, I became aware once more of the immense fortune signified by the fact that they are still in the world. Hence the oft-mentioned "indigenous Knowledge" is not completely lost, but remains alive and active, and—if we have the fortitude necessary—we can venture and seek to establish contact with this Knowledge before it is lost forever. So many legends, tales, and dreams about the Ancient Toltecs. There they were, right in front of my eyes!

I listened, saw, and felt, although what was principally going on between them escaped me. How I wished to be there among them! But not observing—rather participating, comprehending, and sharing the vision of these Toltec survivors. For a moment I surrendered to the absurd frustration of not having been born Wirrarika, to understand their language, to share in their magic feeling toward the world, to be in this same place, another one among them. Quickly I cleared my mind and realized what a gift it meant to be there, receiving with joy that which I could appreciate of a vision such as this.

After a while, the Wirrarika interrupted their rituals and took a break. They also got out tortillas and water and ate a little. One of them approached to talk with us; we told him what we were doing and we spoke a little about the mountain and the communities in which we had been. They were from San Andres. The Wirrarika told us a little about what they were doing on La' Unarre, in the last phase of their Pilgrimage and about to return to the desert. He introduced us to some of his companions and we left open the possibility of meeting again in the mountains. We left them so they could leave the offerings they had brought.

We returned to camp and to the rest of the group who were now awake. Everyone had a faraway and curious look. They had many questions to ask me. I told them there would be time for that. We should remain silent and secluded until the Indians had finished their work. We saw them leave. They passed by and after bidding us farewell, they marched away as they had arrived, walking single file and in silence. I watched until they had disappeared behind a hillside, feeling in my Spirit a kind of indefinite promise. I did not know whether it was a promise coming to me from the outside, or if my heart was expressing it out toward the world. Perhaps it was both things at once.

NINE

THE PILGRIMAGE TO HUMUN' KULLUABY

This is the way that leads to paradise.
We take it, we follow it.

Oh, how beautiful is the peyote flower!
We go to his field
where he was born,
where he hides
like a deer lying
among the grass of paradise.[1]

---

[1] Indigenous song. Taken from a compilation by Fernando Benitez, volume II of *Los Indios de Mexico*, Era publisher.

124 TOLTECS OF THE NEW MILLENNIUM

HEART-STOPPING BEGINNING

Manolo was finally due to arrive in Xonacata, the meeting place agreed upon with the marakame Antonio and the jicareros from Santa Maria. There had been so many last minute difficulties we had to solve in getting an appropriate vehicle to make the trip to Humun' Kulluaby! The truck we had arranged for three months ago had to fail precisely ten hours before departing from Mexico City. Then there were hours of feverish activity trying to get another—the truck rental companies charged very high prices, they couldn't get one on such short notice. Obtaining one from the university or the INI[2] would require bureaucratic time, which we did not have. They were waiting for us! We had promised them a big truck to take them for the Pilgrimage, and if we failed all the Pilgrimage would fail!!

I decided that Manolo should go ahead to Zacatecas to see if professor José Maria Palos of the State University could get us one. The University of Zacatecas and professor Palos in particular have always had an interest in the affairs of the Wirrarika. Meanwhile, the rest of us remained in Mexico City trying by different means to solve the problem. We cannot fail. We have come far to get to this point, then at the eleventh hour, the dream threatens to go up in smoke. There was much at stake: We had a commitment not only with the Wirrarika, but with the Spirit. While I was glued to the telephone in my office making call after call, my mind wavered: "What would happen if we don't . . . ? We would put the entire Pilgrimage in danger!"

The telephone insisted on giving us only negatives. Despair pushed us, trying to take control of our hearts. Internal conviction pushed in the opposite direction. "We can-

---

[2] Instituto Nacional Indigenista, or the Indigenous National Institute

not fail, we cannot fail!" Riiiiiing! Again the telephone took me out of my ruminations.

"Vic! We got a three-ton truck from the University of Zacatecas! I'll leave right away for Mexquitic and go from there to Xonacata."

"Thank God, Manolo! You make my soul return to my body! Get going then and send me one of the guys in Ligia's car to take me from the airport. I'll leave for Zacatecas on the first flight out. Once you're organized, leave me a message with Elvira in the office, telling me where we can find each other."

XONACATA

The old university truck advances lurching down the dirt "road," demanding even for heavy vehicles. Traveling in it are Luis Manuel and Ventura, the university's chauffeur. Given the road and the years of wear and tear on the three-ton, the passengers entrust themselves to their favorite saint for the long trip that awaits them. About twenty meters distant, in a compact car, ride Manolo and one of our friends, also praying that the suspension of the car—and their kidneys—can take the pounding they are receiving.

Manolo attempts to relax by observing the pine forests and breathing the incomparable mountain air. He tries to "tune in" with the surroundings to purge his Spirit of the doubts that now and then nag him inside. What is happening in Xonacata? Will they have waited for us? Will they all fit in the truck?

The uneven road of rocks and holes forms a line in the high part of the sierra. Below, canyons and mountains are seen in the distance. Finally, the fantastic scenery begins to descend toward a beautiful plain surrounded by forest. Xonacata! The sky is separated into blue, red, green, and iridescent orange colors, while the sun hides on the horizon. The souls of my companions feel as if in an inner twilight, announcing the arrival and acquiescence to the mysterious.

Although for them the "Pilgrimage" had begun months ago, the "true grit" was about to begin and this sunset was in their soul, a saying good-bye to the world that would remain behind at the moment when only the Wirrarika Spirit and the designs of Tamatz would count.

Manolo speeds ahead of the bus, trying to make up time. The Nissan's headlights open a little space of light amidst the darkness, which has swallowed everything. The road continues descending until some campfires in the distance promise an imminent arrival. As they advance, hearts start beating more intensely. The dark silhouettes of the Indians outlined against the light of Tatewari make them appear like magic beings—what they are in reality from the moment they started on their way to Humun' Kulluaby. Four campfires warm the pilgrims, some of whom converse quietly. The majority remain silent.

"There are the Wirrarika! They waited for us!"

"But there are a lot of them! It looks like all the jicareros came."

"I think the jicareros are there and many others. There must be more than fifty! We have to find Antonio!"

Around one of the campfires they find Ligia and Armando, who had arrived in another car to join the Pilgrimage with our group. After the hugs and typical greetings, they ask Manolo the whereabouts of the truck, to which he responds with the whole story of the failure of the original and the struggle to get another, which is a little smaller and lagging a little behind.

"Well, here things are a little touchy. The Wirrarika have been quite worried because they have been waiting for hours already. Moreover, there are thirty-three Wirrarika going to Humun' Kulluaby and they are hoping for a very large truck."

"Son of a gun! I calculate the truck will hold no more than twenty-five and a tight fit at that!"

They are embroiled in this when Antonio, the principal marakame and leader of the jicareros, approaches.

"We had problems with the truck, Toño, but don't worry, we got another and it's on its way."

"Very good! Come on over here and we'll sing and dance."

Manolo and the rest go over to the campfire of the Wirrarika, where everyone is gathered. Before beginning to dance and sing, the worried people want to know what had happened to the truck. Seeing the fixed and curious looks of the large group of pilgrims, Manolo proceeds to explain to them the story of the truck and all the complications. Everything is fine until he tells them the truck we finally ended up with will hold only twenty or twenty-five people. Upon hearing this, the Wirrarika change countenance and look seriously worried. The tewaris (mestizos) realize in that moment the delicate responsibility that has been placed into their hands. The truck makes its entrance at that moment and one of the Wirrarika confirms: "Ay! That truck won't hold more than twenty-five and we're thirty-three!" Tayau, a Wirrarika of about thirty years who is distinguished for his fluid use of Spanish, and who in some way is directing the discussion, explains to our group the gravity of the situation:

"You see, the reason they seem so nervous is because each one of them has made a very, very great effort to come here. If one of them after having prepared and begun the Pilgrimage, does not complete it to Humun' Kulluaby, he or she will be fearful and almost surely will become ill or something. For this each one has prepared offerings and each one has a very important motive for going on the Pilgrimage. The jicareros are going to complete their task, which lasts five years; others are going to ask help for a sick member of the family, while others are going to comply with a promise. How can we leave them?"

While Tayau is speaking, a murmur grows among the rest of the Wirrarika, until it becomes a discussion in which many are speaking at the same time. Although the discussion is in Wirrarika, some words in Spanish are sprinkled in, so the

tewaris understand that it has to do with a method of deciding who would remain behind. Some say, "It's okay, I won't
go!" or "I'll stay, let the others go!" Others say, "Let only the
jicareros go! Of course, if we can't all go, let those go who
have to go!" Though they never got angry (I have never seen
an angry Wirrarika), the discussion lasts for almost half an
hour. The tewaris (my friends) feel like complete cockroaches
since they feel responsible for what is happening.

While all this is going on, Antonio, the marakame, and
Luciano, the urukuakame—the oldest and most respected of
the group—lie resting or asleep on the ground, indifferent to
the discussion that is rising in volume.

"Hey, Manolo, why wouldn't it be better to get another
truck so we don't leave anyone behind?" says Tayau.

The tewaris confer and consider this possibility. Con-
clusion: they do not have the means necessary to do it. Oh
well! Manolo cannot help but think what would have happened if he had not been able to get a truck at all.

"I'm very sorry, but there is no way for us to get other
transportation; we've already examined all the possibilities."

For a moment there is silence. After the long discussion
without finding any alternative solution, in one instant the
Wirrarika make a complete about-face in their attitude,
demonstrating fluidity in a direct way and living without the
slavery of self-importance. From a state of anxiety and
extreme preoccupation, they pass to a completely opposite
state by just deciding to do so.

"So that's fine! If we can't all go, then let our council of old
ones (who continue to rest quietly) decide who goes and who
stays!"

Without another word, the Wirrarika set to work. One
takes out a small ritual violin, another brings out a guitar of
similar dimensions, and without any discussion, like a single
body, they begin to dance with a festive and concentrated
spirit. They form a long line with each one close behind the

other. The guitar and the violin begin to play the characteristic melody that accompanies the Wirrarika in all their collective ritual experiences: a short and repetitive melody that nevertheless has an incredible richness. We never tire of hearing it, rather it keeps us content and awake, as though connected to a force coming from who knows where, but intense and good, joyful. It is the same melody that we would hear on the hikes in the desert, in the dances, in the hunt for Hikuri and the deer.

The line of Indians dances around the fire, forming a circle that converts itself into a spiral coming ever closer and closer to Tatewari. When the spiral is almost closed around the fire, the line changes direction and continues the march of the spiral but in reverse. They walk, dancing, backward without turning around for a moment, without running into one another or tripping. At times, one of them yells something in their tongue, and all respond by talking and celebrating, while at the same time there is heard a peculiar whistle made from the tips of a bull's horns, converted into small trumpets. It is announcing the symbolic arrival at one of their sacred places. The dance is rhythmic and intense. Everything is controlled by a synchronization that goes beyond the realm of the merely human: the music, the rhythm, the crackling of the campfire, the night, and the feelings of the men and women who dance around the fire—everything fits together and is a part and an expression of the same instant, in harmony with itself.

The tewaris look on in wonder and accept this lesson that life gave them. They express their admiration and joy by dancing a short distance away without daring to join the line of Indians. When the Wirrarika see they are dancing without stopping, no matter how many hours have passed, they express their pleasure telling them, "That's it! That's how it's done!"

After about three hours the dancing stops, but not the attention. At the fire, one of them begins to shout the names of different sacred places, adding other words in their language, to which the entire group responds with euphoric cries and words of approval. They are blessing all that is important to them and conjuring good fortune for all the pilgrims, and for success in the dangerous crossing they are initiating. At one moment, amidst the Wirrarika words and shouts, the tewaris notice mention of the truck and the two cars, to which are dedicated euphoric words of well-being. Also are blessings for the tewaris, which everyone seconds.

The dance begins once more, and lasts for about two more hours. Afterwards, everyone goes to sleep. The journey to Humun' Kulluaby has begun.

The huge conglomeration of buildings, streets, and con-structions of all kinds shrinks rapidly, until the entire city turns into an enormous lake of concrete. The plane continues to climb, and soon all the scenery below is an interminable carpet of clouds. I close my eyes and try to rest, finally on my way. I did not know what had happened in the mountains, but instinctively I knew that the pieces of the initial chaos would adapt themselves and the natural tendency toward equilibrium would prevail. I mentally run over all the steps that brought me to this point: my walks in the mountains, my encounter with the Wirrarika, my unique experiences in the San Luis desert, my work with the groups.

The Wirrarika have the very clear internal feeling that their life is a path, that each day is a step, and that this path leads to the Spirit. For all my life, since I was a child, I have had this same intuition. Each step, each project, each new adventure, was a step that brought me a little closer to the Source, the Origin. My path came filled with the strangest places, the experiences apparently unrelated. Nevertheless, in spite of their apparent lack of connection, each one of these experiences contained the same unifying substance: the search for my true face, the functional awareness of my link with the Spirit.

Thus were my readings as a child, my first experiences camping out alone or with my friends, my exploration of Mexico, my encounter with the peasants, with the Indians. My incursions into the realm of the mystic, of psychology, of anthropology, and later anti-anthropology. The encounter with the profound Spirit of the Earth. The discovery of the sea and the whales, of communicating with dolphins. The practice of flying in an ultra-light airplane with which I earned my living during the year of my "disappearance." The work groups, courses, conferences in different countries. Traversing the jungle, the desert, the snow-covered mountains, the canyons, the rivers we mounted or descended, dodging rapids. The lakes. The experiences in the world of the *nagual*, the millimetric proximity of death. Writing *The Teachings of Don Carlos*, and later taking responsibility for all the changes it implied.

There had been no years of rest in those years left behind, but their intensity and the soft whispering of the Spirit during each one of them I would not change for anything. Effectively, I direct myself toward the mysterious. I don't know to what world this plane is taking me, but I feel at peace. I have lived the life I wanted, I am not left with desire for anything, and the struggle has been worth the effort. I am ready to die smiling. I am reminded of the song of Cuban poet and singer-author Silvio Rodríguez called "At the End of this Journey", the words, "we remain those who can smile, in the midst of death, in full light, in full light."

I feel happy that I finally am going to Humun' Kulluaby, not as part of some academic investigation, nor as an exotic trip into the world of indigenous folklore, but rather as a step—now inevitable—on my path toward the Spirit. I had heard something in different talks with the Wirrarika, had read about it, and even known first-hand some of the places on the Pilgrimage, but the specific experience of Humun' Kulluaby, which normally only the Wirrarika can witness, was a complete mystery to me. The words of Castaneda's don Juan have a clear and precise meaning for me in this moment: "a man goes to Knowledge as he goes to war: awake, with fear, with respect, and with absolute confidence in himself."

Ah, my dear Wirrarika, even they have fear! There comes to mind that conversation I had with a Wirrarika of around twenty-two years of age.

"Hey Fermin, have you gone to Humun' Kulluaby yet?"

"No, I'm just hanging around making a fool of myself!"

"Why, what's the problem?"

"Because it scares the hell out of me, it's really heavy!"

"But what can happen to you? Besides, isn't it an obligation?"

"Well yes, it is an obligation, but it still scares me. I should have gone three years ago, but here I remain. I just get up enough nerve and at the last minute I chicken out."

"But why the fear?"

"Because it's very tough. Look: one has to go there, to Humun' Kulluaby to view his or her life, to know whether one will be a healer, or dedicated to the land, or be a marakame or whatever. Just the peyote makes me afraid. One has to eat a great deal."

"But you have eaten peyote many times, true? And besides, I see that everyone here has affection for Hikuri, why then so much fear?"

"It's just that there the thing is very different. Look: the key to everything is to confess well. Before entering Humun' Kulluaby one has to confess, telling in front of everyone his or her sins, without leaving anything out. In order to become clean. The problem is that if you don't confess properly, if you hide or forget one, then you can get really screwed up in Humun' Kulluaby or you can have bad luck or get sick. You can even die."

"And what happens with peyote?"

"Well, there is not like here, where you eat a piece of peyote and it helps you to walk or work very pleasantly, listening to the advice of God. There they give you a big pile of it and you have to eat it by force!"

"And if you don't want to eat it all?"

"They hit you! They call into action one or two of what are called sheriffs and they hit you if you don't eat it all, or if you make a gesture they don't like. And quickly, because there are others waiting their turn!"

"And what happens after?"

"Well, anything. It's all in confessing well. If you confess well, then you hear and see Tamatz who speaks to you and tells you everything, everything you need to know. You just sit there listening and seeing. On the other hand, if you do not confess well, later it becomes apparent, because you begin to scream and want to run away. You see devils or any other kind of horrible things."

"And what do they do when this happens to someone? Do they help?"

"They should not help, if it's your fault for not making a good confession. They tie you to a tree or to whatever is handy and let you endure it! Because once it begins, it won't let you go!"

"Wow! Well I can see why it scares you, it would even make me think first!"

"Well, as I've told you, it's all a matter of confessing well. There's a chance I'll go this year and join the jicareros."

After joining my friends and the group of Wirrarika, we advance toward Zacatecas, connection point to the state of San Luis Potosi. We stop by the side of the highway. Finally the whole group of pilgrims is assembled, twenty six jicareros including the marakame. For the tewaris, five will make the trip besides myself. I see that the jicareros are engaged in doing something, since some of them are holding candles with the rest gathered around them. They are speaking in their language.

THE MATEWAMES

Some of the jicareros are covering the faces of the mate-wames ("those who have not seen, but who will see") going to Humun' Kulluaby for the first time. The eldest member Luciano, the urukuakame, with the help of two younger members, places a shawl that covers the head and eyes of the matewames. Of the tewaris, only I have been to Humun' Kulluaby, thus each one of my friends is covered with a ban-danna. I explain to them what I already know of the proce-dure: The shawl that covers the head and partially the eyes (allowing them to see the ground in front of them but not to either side or straight ahead) emphasizes the fact that those who have not been to Humun' Kulluaby *do not truly see* and the fact of having the eyes covered helps them to enter a state of introspection and attention necessary to make the sacred trip bringing them to the paradise of the Wirrarika, which they have had the fortune to visit while alive. They should remain covered until they arrive and have concluded the hunt for the deer-peyote.

I observe the Spirit and attitude of the pilgrims: they are transformed. A feeling of sacredness is felt from their gaze. They look so different from how they look in the mountains. These signs are indicative of the task they are performing. It is not only that they are directing themselves to a place to enter into contact with the Powers that govern the world; rather it is the journey, the traveling itself, they make sacred. They are no longer simply men and women. They have converted them-selves into magic spirits from the moment of the first rituals in the mountains that initiated the Pilgrimage. From this moment, nothing will be the same; everything they do, each step they take, will be a step that allows them to penetrate more and more into the awareness of the other self where the nature of humans becomes one with the nature of the Powers that govern the world.

The matewames lower their heads in an attitude of respect and receive with attention the words of the urukuakame. Ligia, Manolo, René, Luis Manuel, Armando, and myself receive with open hearts those words and gestures, though our reason cannot understand. It is not important to understand. The universal language of feeling unites us more and more to these men and women who, with the passage of days, will be transformed into something much closer: our teokaris, our brothers and sisters. Companions of the journey on this peculiar Pilgrimage toward the Mystery that is life.

Once the matewames have been covered, everyone wishes all a good trip, and we climb into the vehicles. The next stop will be at an indeterminate point, as indicated by Antonio and Luciano, to spend the night and to face one of the key moments of the Pilgrimage: the confession.

Antonio travels now in the front part of the truck, together with Luciano. They scrutinize the darkness looking for some sign that would indicate to them the precise place to stop. Forty minutes past our previous stop, something makes them pause. In spite of the darkness, I manage to observe that we are stopped on a flat zone with semi-desert vegetation. Once the motors are shut off, the sounds of the night help us to locate where we really are. Although we find ourselves on the edge of the highway, the sound of passing vehicles is practically nil. With or without the highway, the Wirrarika occupy the world with the same attitude of respect and confidence that is so much their own. After all, they were here long before the highway and the tewaris. There is no moon, only the favored company of the stars sprinkles the darkness.

THE NIGHT OF THE WIRRARIKA

The group moves farther from the belt of asphalt to place themselves a sufficient distance from the road. The handbags and small bundles of the Wirrarika begin to work their magic and from them come small logs, all nearly the same size and diameter. In a few minutes, they have prepared a fire in which the logs, like arrows, all point toward the east, the region where Tau (the Sun) appears. Before lighting Tatewari (the Fire), Luciano speaks to him. He asks that he accept the food they have brought for him. That he continue to protect them during the long journey ahead. With the feeling that we sense in his words and the deep emotion in his gaze, we realize that his love for Tatewari, which he has cultivated all his life, is in no way figurative, but is an active force, powerful, alive. Luciano brings a match close and as though this small flame had opened a door to another world, an enormous blaze is produced in a instant. Each one of us present has a small log or branch; it is our offering to the Grandfather Fire. Before placing them, all the pilgrims shout at once the names of their sacred places, toward which they point a log or branch, as though it were an arrow, invoking the powers of each place. "Rapaviyame! (Lake Chapala), Aurramanaka! (the temple of the Earth, in Durango), Aramara! (the coast of San Blas), Humun' Kulluaby!" After each name there follows a generous amount of festive and affectionate phrases, uttered by all simultaneously. Once the power of the sacred places has been summoned, the pilgrims approach the fire to surrender their pieces of wood, at which time they speak to it. Immediately afterward, the Wirrarika remove from their handbags a small quantity of corn flour, and deposit it in the fire at the same time, never without neglecting to speak to it.

EL KAWITERO

One of the jicareros named Juan, about fifty years old, begins to speak with much force and grand gestures in front of the fire. He speaks very fast, provoking much laughter from all. Later, he begins to speak more softly until he falls asleep and begins to snore, which is entertaining to everyone.

We tewaris do not understand what is going on. The man begins his litany again with new force, pointing to the fire, to the distance, to the people, and soon he begins to cry intensely! To our surprise, nobody is worried, in fact they laugh shamelessly; the more intense the groans and sobbing words of the man, the more intense their laughter. I approach Tayau, who is in charge of informing us of the parts we do not understand and of giving us instructions that we might lack. With a gesture I ask what's going on.

"He's kawiteing!"

"Whaaaaat?"

"He is the kawitero and he is relating the history of the world!"

At that moment I understand what has occurred and I explain it to my companions. The kawitero is doing a satire of the actual kawitero.[3] He is parodying Luciano, who is probably having more fun than anyone. Juan is pretending to be asleep, one of the worst things that could happen to a kawitero. The laughing gets to the highest level when Juan makes a ridiculous representation of the weeping and tears that the actual kawitero usually does during the telling of the Sacred History. For close to an hour they continue the kawito and the laughter. Next come the impersonations and changing names.

CHANGING NAMES

Antonio, Luciano, and Julio proceed to hand out roles that are at the same time real and fictitious responsibilities. Thus they named sheriffs, secretaries, judges, treasurers, administrator, commandant, and anything else they could think of, the important thing being that everyone is assigned a role. The last to receive his role is our friend, René who, as they couldn't think of anything else, is named president. They call him Carlos Salinas de Gortari, which everyone celebrates with laughter and jokes. As roles are assigned they pretend not to want them and then have to be convinced. Occasionally, people take off running and the sheriffs have to give chase and catch them, until they finally accept. They also change the name of everything—the tortillas, the water, the handbags, the offerings, the sky, the earth, the fire, the cars, including the persons who have already acquired names distinct from their real names. The new names will be used until the Pilgrimage is over. The sheriffs are charged with making sure that no one

---

[3] The kawitero is the eldest person in the jicareros group, who has the responsibility of telling the Story of the World during the Pilgrimage.

makes a mistake and with imposing a fine on the violator. At the same time everyone else keeps an eye on the sheriffs, to make sure they didn't make a mistake. I realize that this changing names is not only a game but also a very efficient way of maintaining the work of attention, and principally a way of emphasizing the nonordinary character of everyone and everything that occurs during the Pilgrimage.

THE DANCE OF THE JICAREROS

After changing names comes the dance of the jicareros. Similar to what they did in Xonacata, they march in single file around the fire forming a spiral, which, at a mere signal, begins walking backward. Julio is always in the line playing his little guitar, and Galindo his violin. Together they make music that produces a state I would dare qualify as "hypnotic" while at the same time alert and joyful. On this occasion they add a very beautiful variation: At times, when the spiral is almost completely closed around the fire, the first one in line turns around and begins to walk facing front but in the opposite direction to those just arriving, in such a way that one part of the line moves inward while the other moves outward, without loss of order or synchronization at any moment. From time to time the bullhorns are sounded, followed by joyful cries on the part of the dancers. They shout the names of the sacred places and make mention of their wonders. Through having observed and participated in it many times, I realize the dance is in reality a representation of the jicarero's task, which means traveling constantly to the many distant sacred sites and bringing offerings from one site to another, always with Tatewari at the center of everything. The dance of the jicareros not only produces profound states of heightened awareness when practiced for hours, but it also reaffirms the internal conviction they have in carrying out their tasks as well as consolidating the Spirit of the group.

THE CONFESSION

Finally arrives the hour so feared by the tewaris: the confession. The reason for our uneasiness is not the difficulty in making our intimate affairs public, but that these are moments outside of ordinary reality, in front of our teokaris, and most important of all, the confession is done before Tatewari, who cannot be fooled. What made us uncomfortable each time the topic of confession came up was the difficulty in assimilating the meaning that the Wirrarika give the word "sin." As far as I knew, we had to mention aloud each of the persons with whom we had had sexual relations during our life, which often means referring explicitly to amorous encounters with a women or man who is also one of those present at the confession. This aroused certain controversy among us. Some made it plain they were at a loss because they did not consider their sexual encounters to be "sins" and therefore did not know whether they could confess other things that carried more weight for them. My position was that there was no reason to speculate on what the word sin might mean to the Wirrarika, but one fact we could not ignore: This was how they confessed and we were in their world and their methods and ways were law; therefore our personal considerations would have to be laid aside, in order to confess exactly as do the Wirrarika. We did agree in any case that in addition to confessing "Wirrarika style," we could also—if we felt the need—confess some other matter that was weighing us down internally. As always happens, concrete reality ended up giving us the answers our speculations never could have.

Those first to confess are the marakame and the urukuakame. We are all seated in silence around the fire. At a given moment, the sheriffs grab hold of Luciano and bring him before the fire, exhorting him to confess his sins without leaving out a single one. Luciano begins to relate the chain of his sins committed during his long life. His amorous encounters must have been many, for he takes a long time. Each time we hear him mention the name of a woman, the sheriffs repeat it in a loud voice, while another jicarero makes a knot in a small rope. When the telling of his sins is finished, he ends it by saying something like, "May the Grandfather Fire purge me of my sins," dusting off his clothes at the same time as though removing something undesirable from himself. In that moment all respond aloud: "Thus it shall be." The rope with the knots is thrown in the fire.

The marakame follows, then one by one the rest of the Wirrarika confess in a similar way, saying in a loud voice the names of their different sexual partners. No one escapes the confession; men and women do it all the same, regardless of age or the fact that they are in the company of their husbands or wives. At certain times, we notice by their tone of voice that the elements of the confession touch very sensitive fibers in the pilgrims.

Judging by the long lists of some of those present, we might get the impression that they are very sensual, although when our turn came, we found we were not in reality at all distinct from them, the difference being that they take upon themselves the task of reporting it to the community, whereas we do not.

One curious thing occurred in order to offset the difficulties of the situation: as the confessors take their turns, they feign trying to escape and the sheriffs bring—sometimes drag—them back to the fire. While they are confessing, if there is the least hesitation or if they remain mute, the sheriffs hit them with a belt, pressuring them to confess everything. All of this has a meaning; it involves laughter and a sense of humor that, nevertheless, does not diminish in any way the profound significance of this part of the Pilgrimage. In fact, the success of the Pilgrimage depends on the degree to which the pilgrims "cleanse themselves."

The hours pass and there are still many confessions to go. It is evident that no one will sleep that night. I am seated strategically next to Tayau and now and then he translates part of the confessions for me, so I better understand the proceedings. Thus I become aware that—given that the Wirrarika live in the country—their confessions not only include people but occasionally goats and cows, and masturbation is also a topic touched upon. It is evident the confession has to be very honest, without leaving out any matters having to do with sex.

"You have to confess well, Victor! Sure, it takes effort, but it's the only way to come out clean and complete so you can go to Humun' Kulluaby. Better to let everything out that has to come out and afterward we'll all be clean and so content!"

At this point I summon up my courage and resolve to confront my destiny. I know what is at stake and I can't go about with half-closed eyes. A curious thing happens when the confessions begin. I had seated myself so that my turn would be one of the last, in order to observe first and act later. How surprising it is when I realize that, while we have the custom of beginning by going around to the right, the Wirrarika are accustomed to go the left. Thus in wanting to be one of the last I end up being one of the first and I am the first of the tewaris to confess.

When the sheriffs come for me I arise very determined, but hardly am I in front of the fire when I feel something I had never imagined: I remain mute! With great difficulty I manage to say: "Before you, Grandfather Fire, and before all my teokaris, I confess that . . ." Then begins an internal battle to remember my sexual encounters, beginning with those during adolescence. The sensation is beyond the world of words. In my insides a great quantity of energy is swirling and stirring, involving emotions, experiences, fears, pain, as well as joys and delights, all struggling to get out at the same time, while reason fights against the "amnesia." Each time I mention a name, the sheriffs repeat it so all can hear and one more knot is added to the rope of my life. I continue for a while with this internal and external struggle. I truly want to tell everything, there is nothing I wish to hold back, but my capacity for verbalization is very far from the intensity I am experiencing inside. Antonio must have realized what is happening to me because after a while he tells me, "Give a number! If there are many of them, give a number!" Thanks, Antonio, I thought, for getting me out of this place of torments. I give a number that I feel corresponds to what I have omitted and even manage to voice before the fire a couple of matters that affect me very deeply and need to be liberated.

I truly feel renewed, with a kind of very special internal cleanliness. I do not feel content or euphoric or sad. I feel different, as if my perception of myself is not that with which I am normally familiar. What "I" am in this moment is of another nature—one who perceives the world with a type of profound silence and who knows perfectly well where he is going and what he is doing in that place and specific moment of the world, although he cannot express or comprehend it rationally. I realize that the meaning of the word "sin" has nothing to do with moral considerations, but rather with energetic ones exclusively. The procedure is impeccable, exactly what is required to be able to tune in to the appropriate frequency for the trip to Humun' Kulluaby.

Wirrarika and tewaris confess one by one. As my friends each take their turn, I observe with pleasure and admiration the fortitude they demonstrate in the face of such a demanding moment. Without doubt they have prepared adequately and won by sheer hard work their place in the Pilgrimage.

TAU

The night wears on and by first light we pilgrims are clean. By dawn, a euphoria takes hold of all those present. Tau is greeting the travelers and blessing them once more with his light and heat! The joy floods all, since this light is felt as a presage of what is waiting for us in Humun' Kulluaby. The pilgrims receive the sun while dancing around the fire. The intensity of the jubilant expressions increases. We are going to Humun' Kulluaby, we are going to the encounter with Tamatz! What joy!

After the dance, all gather around very close together, with the marakame (representing the Sun) in the center. Holding his muvieri aloft and shaking it, he utters words having to do with the unity of the jicareros and their total commitment. A rope is passed around everyone, as a symbol representing the spiritual cohesion of the group. The cleansing of the confession and our union toward the same objective establish optimum conditions for entering Humun' Kulluaby.

At around eight in the morning some food is brought. Before taking a bite, as is the custom of the Wirrarika, they give a small part to the fire. "Tatewari first!" after which they offer food to the sacred places and finally we eat.

During the trip we eat once a day. The pilgrim diet is very austere: tortillas and water. On some occasions there are refreshments, if we happen to pass close to a town or ranch. On every occasion all of us share our food with the rest. After breakfast, we take to the highway again, this time going to Zacatecas, and from there toward San Luis Potosi.

The appearance of the Pilgrimage is very picturesque. At the head is the university truck replete with feathered Wirrarika and an occasional tewari. Although the truck supposedly had sides, the sides measured less than a meter high, so the passengers are not only crowded together, but also in a constant effort to maintain equilibrium. It is worthy of comment that in spite of traveling this way for hours on end, not once does a single pilgrim complain; rather they display contentment and good humor at all times. Behind the truck are the two little compact cars—long since covered with dust and betraying the first signs of giving out—bearing some sloppily dressed tewaris, in addition to water, oranges, blankets, and many other things.

The highway patrolman who pulls one of the cars over for having crossed the center line in a no-passing zone is curious when he observes the passengers with their heads and eyes covered. Fortunately, he is understanding when the reason is explained to him and he sees the university truck filled with strange-looking passengers.

Once in the state of San Luis, we direct ourselves to a town on the edge of the desert, where the Wirrarika supply themselves with a large amount of necessary items: small mirrors, candles, chocolate, small jugs that later would become very important, and similar things. Without knowing how these things are to be used, we tewaris also provide ourselves with similar objects "just in case."

The moment arrives when we have to abandon the highway and enter the desert; we are still around one hundred fifty kilometers—which we will have to travel practically cross country—from Humun' Kulluaby.

We now find ourselves in open desert. All that can be seen around us is a gray-colored flatness, sprinkled with small bushes and now and then some type of nopal. The cars now are feeling—as the saying goes—what it means "to love God in the land of the Indians." The truck, on the other hand, keeps a slow but sure pace. We are able to do the first few kilometers of the desert in a relatively straight line, down a path where the earth is flat and free of bushes. Now and then the route crosses with other paths and the urukuakame has to decide which is better. At this point the usual references have no meaning. Everything looks the same on all sides. After having covered about forty or fifty kilometers during which the path becomes gradually rougher, we stop at a place that does not appear to be anything special.

THE FOOD FOR TATEWARI

The Wirrarika step off the truck and quickly get to work. They place their meager "baggage," forming a circle around a place indicated by the marakame. There is heard the characteristic sound of the bullhorns and at the same time the majority of the jicareros—this time without Luciano and Antonio—form a line and go off into the desert. They take us so much by surprise that only some of us tewaris manage to join. Around a third of the Wirrarika remain as well.

The column advances with a synchronization they never lose. Now and then, one of them sounds a bullhorn and the others respond by sounding theirs, along with jubilant cries, without slackening the pace. The music of the guitar and violin is always present, bestowing a festive air to the moment.

Always when the memory of these walks comes to mind, or of the dance of the jicareros and what I felt from having participated in them, I am amazed how among the Wirrarika, they produce a peculiar state that I have not seen anywhere else. This state has to do with the meaning of the word "fiesta," which for us usually implies mirth with "laxity"—the dispersion of attention. I remember my surprise years ago when I observed that they often called their most profound rituals "fiestas," speaking of the fiesta of the corn, the fiesta of the drum, and so forth. As I got to know and participate in the different rituals, I could see that for them the experience of the fiesta is very different from ours. Their state is without a doubt festive and joyful, but different from the soirees of modern people. Their attention is not dispersed; on the contrary, it increases. The result is that while they are very joyful, they never fall into laxity. They place themselves into states of high concentration and heightened awareness, without solemnity but with joy. These states of joy could and did alternate with others—instantly and totally—into states of profound sadness or silent contemplation, since the Wirrarika are masters of the art of fluidity and they have no difficulty in changing their attention the moment it becomes necessary. Their long walks are like this as well: no talking, a rhythm and harmony in which everyone's attention is united around the penetrating, repetitive (but not monotonous), and joyful sound of the violin and the guitar, to which occasionally is added the jubilant sound of the bullhorns.

The procession arrives at a small tree about two meters in height with abundant branches, and they begin to move around in a circle with the tree in the center. It is evident they are dancing for the tree. After about twenty minutes the dancing and music stop. The jicareros play their bullhorns one more time. One of them approaches the tree and begins to speak to it with a great deal of seriousness for some minutes; at times his speech turns very affectionate and emotional to the point of tears. When he finishes, he cuts off one of the branches, a small bough of about forty centimeters, from which he strips all the bark. He sharpens the point like an arrow, then he points the arrow toward the four directions while praying for the Spirit of the tree. All those present join their voices in as well. At this point, they approach the tree, cut it down, then proceed to chop it into small pieces of the same size, from which they also remove the bark. In an incredibly short span of time, there remains no trace of the tree while each Wirrarika has in hand a bit of food for Tatewari. The group turns to go back.

Soon it is getting dark and the urukuakame lights the fire, following all the necessary steps for the invocation of Tatewari. We all participate in a way similar to that already described in the night of the confession. When everything is ready Antonio asks us tewaris to go to sleep since what is to follow pertains only to the Wirrarika. I ask him if we can walk a little and he says yes but to take care. We take the opportunity to practice one of our favorite activities when we are in uninhabited areas: walking in the dark without flashlights or candles. Its practice has taught me that, if carried out correctly, the walking increases our attention, allowing unusual means of bodily perception to come to the fore, while sight plays a secondary role. In this way, we can walk quite securely and integrate ourselves fully with the world of shadows.

We move some distance from the campsite, and merge ourselves into the nocturnal perception of the desert. After about three or four kilometers, we select an appropriate site and sit on the ground, forming an energetic circle with our backs to the inside, our faces out. Seated in this way we unite our attention and have a 360-degree perception of the surrounding desert. Later we bend our heads backward until they touch, and we unify our perception of the stars. We remain about an hour in this position without talking. After that we speak a little about our situation in very low tones, so as not to disturb the energetic condition of the surroundings. Finally we turn to go back, this time running at top speed for the pure pleasure of moving in the dark. We realize that our bodies are asking for something intensely physical. Before arriving at the campsite, we steady our breathing and once again become quiet.

We arrive in silence and the Wirrarika seem not to notice us. They are talking around the fire, one at a time while the others listen. It is not an ordinary conversation; they are occupied with some topic of real importance. Later we become aware they are deliberating on which steps and route to follow in the days to come. Half an hour passes, then everyone goes to bed. It is around two in the morning.[4]

TATEI MATINIERI

When I wake the following morning, I find the Wirrarika piling their things on the truck. Rapidly we hurry to pack ours since I assume we will leave immediately for Humun' Kulluaby. To my surprise, however, once the things are on the truck, the pilgrims instead of climbing on, form a long line, which this time includes everyone. We proceed to join, very curious as to the destination and purpose of the hike. The bullhorns sound and the procession marches off. After a short

---

[4] Regarding that night in which apparently "nothing happened"— Tayau told us, during a trip to the mountains we made three months later, that it was a very important night since it was then the marakame Antonio opened the "door" giving access to Humun' Kulluaby. While everyone else slept, he went to the fire and spoke to it, after which he waited for the deer antlers to appear. When that happened he took them between his hands and brought them out from the fire, indicating that we could enter Humun' Kulluaby and hunt for Hikuri.

time walking, we arrive at a town or ranch composed of only a few adobe houses and others of white brick. The unpaved ground is no different than that of the rest of the desert. The few townspeople do not seem surprised at the presence of the long and picturesque line of pilgrims, which makes me think that the town is on the normal route of the Pilgrimage. We continue along until we cross the town and in a short time arrive at a rectangular area around 300 meters square surrounded by wire mesh on all four sides. Inside is a mesquite, another tree I can't identify, and assorted bushes. Apart from the fence, the only peculiarity of the area is its greenness, which contrasts with the desert. The fence has a small door where the pilgrims enter. Upon entering I manage to read a sign from the National Indigenous Institute that says the place is a ceremonial temple of the Wirrarika, entry is prohibited, and littering or allowing entry of animals would be grounds for a large fine or arrest by the competent authorities. I realize we are in one of the most important places on the way to Humun' Kulluaby.

As the Wirrarika enter, they sit down on the ground, squatting over their calves or with their legs crossed. I discover the reason for the greenness and agreeable freshness of the place: we are in Tatei Matinieri, a spring that wells up in the middle of the desert. This is one of those places where dwells the Lady of the Water so venerated by the Wirrarika people. (She also inhabits Lake Chapala in Jalisco and the coasts of San Blas, Nayarit.)

I have heard a lot about Tatei Matinieri. Each time the Wirrarika refer to this place, they do it with grand emotion, describing it as one of the most beautiful places in the world. And Tatei Matinieri certainly is beautiful, not only due to the presence of the water, which had formed a small stream, or the few trees. It was something deep and ineffable that made us feel so good there. Entering Tatei Matinieri is like crossing into another dimension, in which the heat and severe aspect of the desert become only a memory. Here I feel comforted, protected, and enveloped in the love of the Lady of the Water.

Once the Wirrarika are seated, they take colored bandannas out of their bags and lay them out on the ground at the edge of the spring. On the bandannas are placed a large quantity of offerings. In a short time the pilgrims have in front of them an altar presenting to Tatei Matinieri the richest offerings: candles, arrows, deer antlers, chocolate, cookies, coins, nierikas, god's eyes, corn of different colors, peyote, feathered arrows, embroidery, and many other things. Once more was proved that out of the handbag of a Wirrarika can come anything, without regard to weight or size. We also place our offerings and remain silent, like all our teokaris.

Antonio begins the ritual, talking to Tatei Matinieri in a language that—although it was Wirrarika—we understand without difficulty, since it is overflowing with love, affection, and gratitude. He does not speak as one would to an omnipotent and distant god, but as if to someone very, very close. He brings out several small bottles of water and, with the point of his muvieri, sprinkles a few drops of water from each one into the water pouring from the spring. Each small bottle contained water that Antonio himself had gathered from the coast of San Blas and from Lake Chapala that he carefully kept for occasions such as this one. Then, kneeling at the edge of the water, he places some of his offerings in the water while he speaks to it with eyes full of tears. Next, Luciano approaches the water and conducts himself in a way similar to Antonio. The rest of the pilgrims place some offerings while speaking to the Spirit of the water—colored arrows wound with colored yarn, mirrors, lit candles on the edge of the water, and other objects.

Then, Antonio, Luciano, and two other jicareros pass to the other side of the stream. The pilgrims follow, placing themselves next to them five rows wide by five rows deep. They kneel down with heads bowed; if they are matewames they momentarily remove the shawls covering their heads and wait their turn. The jicareros are helping draw water from the stream. They bring it to Antonio and Luciano, who wet the feathers of their muvieri and sprinkle water on the head of each person, uttering words that emphasize the sacred character of the water of Tatei, as imbued in the pilgrims. The state of grace into which they enter upon contact with the water of Tatei reaches its maximum when, upon finishing speaking, the marakame or urukuakame empties the cup completely, literally bathing the pilgrim, who receives it laughing and rubbing it on his or her head and body. When my turn nears, I approach Tayau.

"Hey Tayau! Why do the Wirrarika love so much Tatei Matinieri?"

His clean and profound gaze along with his broad smile gives me the answer as his words corroborate: "Tatei Matinieri are the eyes of our Mother the Earth!"

I reel internally upon realizing the true dimension of what we are doing. I feel a love and an enormous respect for these men and women living in an intimate relation with the Earth. They are giving us, through their example, the opportunity to learn what it means to be real people able to understand, live, and reflect love for the Earth.

I place myself in position while my entire field of energy stirs with pleasant expectation. I feel the voice of the marakame, the force of his muvieri, and the internal freshness taking hold of my being when the first drops touch my head. A true blessing. The stream of water bathes me and I feel the wonder of being alive, the privilege of sharing this incomparable world alongside such human beings as these, enchanted with love for the Earth and with the greatest mystery of all— to be alive still!

After bathing in the waters of Tatei Matinieri, my eyes truly open so that I see what we are. We are not Wirrarika, nor tewaris, nor Indians, nor mestizos. We are fields of energy on their way to the mysterious. We are the same! No one is better or worse! We are teokaris and we are together because the same light is calling us! The water of the eyes of the Earth are intermingled with water from my own. I turn around to look at my teokaris and I see they are all the same. We are ready to go to Humun' Kulluaby!

We pilgrims continue to place our offerings. We set aside a little, then surrender ourselves to an encounter with Tatei Matinieri and speak to her of the multiple feelings that turn around inside our souls as a consequence of this amazing trip called life. We ask for her light, her advice, and her force. Some cry intensely upon opening their hearts to the Lady of the Waters. The Lady of the Waters responds to us and heals us.

Before leaving, we take the small jugs we purchased on the way and fill them with holy water, which we can use when the appropriate moment arrives. With full jugs and full hearts, we prepare to depart. Antonio approaches the truck and asks that the hood be raised. With his muvieri, he sprinkles some of the water just collected over the motor. He does the same with the cars. Now I have no doubt the vehicles will withstand the trip. We get in the truck and the cars. On to Humun' Kulluaby!

HUMUN' KULLUABY

The road becomes more difficult as we go on. In fact, there are no roads, only very narrow paths crossing on all sides in the desert; to the sides, spiny bushes give the owners of the cars a hard time. This is a true labyrinth, which lasts hours longer than expected. When I ask Antonio if there is much more to go he says "Soon." Finally night falls. We go a little farther, and the urukuakame decides we should make camp again, since in the dark it would be impossible to find "the place." Conversing with the jicareros confirms what had become apparent to me—for them it also was difficult to locate Humun' Kulluaby. Even the oldest, who have come innumerable times during their lives, have to struggle on each occasion to orient themselves in the desert and find the specific site indicated by tradition. On this occasion there are no dances or rituals. We only rest hoping that Tau will appear again, allowing us to find the road. What cannot be dispensed with is the presence of Tatewari, without which the Wirrarika would feel helpless, so they rapidly light a fire, which watches over our sleep until dawn.

As soon as the sun shows on the horizon, activity commences—the dance of the jicareros around the fire. Since we have been in the desert, the nights have been much colder and at this hour we are still numb, so a good dance seems most appropriate. They form the habitual line, sound the bullhorns, and let the notes of the violin and guitar be heard. We tewaris also dance. Each time we comprehend better the internal meaning of these dances, only now I feel so close to my Wirrarika brothers that I feel ridiculous dancing outside the line. Without thinking about it more, I enter the line of Wirrarika, just behind Antonio, whom I've known for a long time. To my surprise, all the Wirrarika are delighted, making gestures of approval, causing the rest of the tewaris to also join the line of dancers.

At this point in the trip we are all equally dusty and the distinction between tewaris and Wirrarika, which was apparent at the beginning, is gradually disappearing. Now that we dance together, I understand many details that had escaped me in the dance of the jicareros. We are representing the trip to the sacred places. The sounds of the bullhorns are heard. "Now we arrive at Rapaviyame!" "Hurrah!" they all respond. "Now I am seeing Lake Chapala! And I even see the little boats!" The dance continues for a long time; the effort to make the appropriate dance steps, keeping the correct distance from the ones ahead and behind, places us in a state of increased awareness. Especially when we dance backward, without turning to the side, it is necessary to "feel" the dancer behind, following in the same manner as before when we followed the one ahead. Heading the line is Julio, playing his violin. His music urges us on so, we could follow him indefinitely, no matter where.

After greeting the day dancing, we feel alert and in the best of spirits, ready to continue our search. The dance this morning broke the barriers between Wirrarika and tewaris, to the point where I ask myself if they had ever existed or were only a product of our imagination. Later Antonio would tell me that we shouldn't be in doubt about participating in every-thing, since that is precisely what they expect from us. If the jicareros had accepted us, we were accepted completely; there was no need to hesitate.

The state of attention in which the entire group of pilgrims find themselves is not an ordinary state. A feeling prevails of looking for something very valuable, but at the same time very evasive. Although there is conviction in the heart, no one would say the battle is won. The trip to Humun' Kulluaby has never been considered an easy one. The uncertainty of the matewames grows and at times they doubt if they really will arrive at that mythical place of which they have heard so many marvelous things. With every step we seem to get fur-ther away. After an hour of advancing through the desert, we get the impression the area is divided into squares by paths that appear from all directions, offering many possibilities at once. The guides do the best they can while the cars face great difficulties with the terrain. The paths are like two canals through which the tires pass, and between them is a "rib" that often scrapes the bottom of the cars. At many points we have to get out since the cars get stuck. Toward the edge of the paths there is no possibility as they are full of spiny bushes. We put up with it and keep going; we well know we haven't come here for a day in the country. Now and then we come across small settlements that look as though they are populat-ed by phantoms. I wonder what the people here could do for a living. It just so happens that one of the most solitary dwellings is called "the souls," from which we can imagine all sorts of things.

Unexpectedly the truck stops. We get down to see what happened. One of the Wirrarika says, "We've arrived at

Humun' Kulluaby!" I look around but I don't see any difference between this and the countryside through which we
have been passing. The Wirrarika lay their things in a small
clearing free of bushes where there is at least one mesquite
tree (there is always one at sacred sites), and this seems to me
to be special since we have seen no other mesquite since Tatei
Matinieri. I look at the place, trying to observe what makes it
different from the rest of the desert. I find empty sardine cans,
a few pop bottles, and a little other garbage. Under a bush at
the edge of the clearing, I also discover peyote cactus planted
in a special order, giving the impression of being an altar. Also
there are the remains of a fire and some wood piled up.
Obviously the place has been visited recently. Antonio tells
me that all the jicarero groups come here each year, to the
same site in the same season. On this occasion those from
Santa Maria were the last to come to hunt the deer.

Once "installed," the jicareros bring out sacks, handbags,
and other bags of various types. Also they carry a knife or a
jackknife. Preparing ourselves for what is to come, we do the
same. I ask Tayau:

"What's next?"

"We hunt deer!" he answers.

We form a line and, with the blowing of the horns and
under the spell of the musical instruments, we advance, alert.
We follow one of the many paths, walking several kilometers
from the campsite. The urukuakame indicates for us to stop.
Antonio steps to one side of the line and all turn to watch him.
He takes out his muvieri and points it outward toward the
field of desert, moving his arm slowly, covering the area in
front of him. He begins to speak as if praying, while indicating with his muvieri in which directions the hunt of the deer
will be carried out. Tayau explains the instructions to us—we
should spread the line out, separating ourselves from the
companion on either side, and begin to comb the area indicated by Antonio, searching for the little deer (peyote). Nobody
should pick a single one until someone has found a family of

Hikuris resembling the figure of a deer. At that point, the marakame casts an arrow at the Hikuri-deer and with this the hunt begins. Then everyone should pick as many Hikuris as they can find and carry. To be the first to find the Hikuri in the form of a deer would be a sign of good fortune for the one who should be so lucky. Before starting we all cut a small branch from the surrounding bushes and rub it over our bodies to protect us against any unpleasant small animals we might encounter during the hunt.

THE HUNT FOR PEYOTE

The horns sound once more and the marakame, who is in front, makes a signal with his arrows. All at once, the line about eighty meters long advances to one side of the path, thus beginning the search. The arrangement of the line that Antonio showed us is very appropriate for "sweeping" the area inch by inch, similar to that used by the Wirrarika in the sierra to corral and hunt "real" deer.

At last we are in Humun' Kulluaby, combing the ground, searching for Hikuri. Although our tewari purpose was not the eating of the sacred cactus, given our norm of going ahead according to how circumstances dictate, we join the hunt with total concentration. My idea is that all the peyote my friends and I can gather would make a very useful gift to the community of Santa Maria, which required it for the many "fiestas" celebrated throughout the year.

The minutes pass and it seems no one has found a single Hikuri. Everyone walks alone, selecting the route that seems best. When I encounter my friends I ask them with a gesture how it is going. "Nothing," they answer with another gesture. I continue my search, looking at every inch of ground. I begin to ask myself if, with so many years of coming to the same site, the Wirrarika had exhausted the peyote reserves. I realize my attention is dispersing in vain speculations and I remember what I had learned years earlier with other Wirrarika friends. I change my state of anxiety for one of relaxation. I silence my thoughts and immediately there appears before me an enormous Hikuri just to my left about a meter. I turn around and see a Wirrarika picking a cactus, making me think they already have found the peyote in the shape of a deer. I continue quietly although ten more minutes pass without finding another. I begin to sing my old peyote songs, and now finding many Hikuri does not seem to matter much, or even finding none at all. I am in the house of Tamatz[5] and his power is felt everywhere with or without cactus. As soon as I am content, cactus begins to appear everywhere. Here there are three together. I bend down to pick them, first asking their pardon for cutting off their lives. I explain to them that the Wirrarika need them to look for Tamatz. I feel that they understand. I pay a lot of attention, cutting them with great care, leaving the root in the earth so another Hikuri will grow in its place.

I continue with my hunt and soon my bag is full. I see that my friends have also found some, although not all have had the same luck. One of them has found only two or three. "Don't be discouraged," I tell him. "The amount is not important." I look at the Wirrarika and some of them already have a sack full. "My goodness! How do they do it?" Our friend Tayau travels with his young wife Alicia. She always carries at her breast or on her back their small son less than a year old. She participates together with her baby in the hunt for the deer like any other pilgrim. For certain they have gathered quite a bit of peyote. Surely the majority of the Wirrarika have come to these places since they were infants, as well. Unlike city dwellers who search for the experience of psychedelic plants, the Wirrarika do not have chaotic hallucinations. Thanks to their characteristic rituals, which include the consumption of peyote and a lifetime of preparation, they are able to perceive a world with internal coherence and continuity, although of a nature very different from the ordinary world.

---

[5] Tamatz, Tamatzin of Tamatz Kahullumary, is the Blue Deer, representation of the Great Spirit.

THE MAN WHO ATTRACTED PEYOTES

I see Antonio there, carrying an enormous sack of peyote, which he can hardly carry. My full handbag now seems much smaller. I stay glued to him to see if I can unravel the secret that allows the Wirrarika to find Hikuri with such apparent ease. I walk behind him. Wherever he walks, there is Hikuri! It seems they are coming out to meet him!

"Hey Antonio, what do you do to find so much Hikuri?"

"Well, it's right there, all you have to do is look!"

"To look?" I continue close behind him and look. Nothing.

"What's the matter, why didn't you pick these up?" asks Antonio who has stopped to watch me.

"Which ones?"

"Those right next to you!"

I scrutinize the ground. "Where?"

Antonio comes over and points to a place about forty centimeters from my feet.

"Right here!"

I can't get over my amazement. "But I've been over this place about four times and there was nothing!"

"Well how could that be, if there it is. Go on now, pick it up."

Near Antonio where Hikuri "appears" on all sides, I soon fill the other bag I carry with me, and help him fill his second sack.

When he feels that is enough, the marakame turns toward an enormous desert plant. It has a trunk similar to a palm tree and in the upper part some large yellow leaves that make it appear like a giant flower. Upon it are hung a few handbags and already the jicareros are gathering around. The bullhorns are sounded and soon the remainder of the pilgrims appear.

THE HOUR OF THE MATEWAMES

Once they are reunited, they prepare an altar by placing several shawls on the ground. Upon these are placed deer antlers, woolen yarn paintings with motifs relating to the

Pilgrimage, corn, and a large quantity of peyote. Each pilgrim lights a candle held in the left hand, while the marakame and the urukuakame begin with prayers and invocations, which everyone follows with concentration. Touching with the eagle feathers of his muvieri, Antonio blesses all the offerings on the altar, as well as all those present. His words are very different from the normal language of the Wirrarika; they seem more like a song.

While Antonio proceeds with his labor to propitiate the Powers that inhabit Humun' Kulluaby, some of the jicareros peel the peyote and cut it into small pieces. The hour of truth is near for the matewames.

When there are enough pieces, designated jicareros begin passing out the small chunks of Hikuri. Before placing it in the mouth of each pilgrim, they place it on the forehead, on the eyes, over the ears, and over the heart in order "to see, to hear, to feel." Each Wirrarika solemnly receives a small piece of peyote, which they eat in silence. The matewames, going for the first time, receive a bowl overflowing with a large quantity of peyote. I receive with respect and gratitude my little piece of Hikuri and the blessings of Antonio. Later with curiosity I observe my friends confronting, for the first time, the very strong and bitter taste of peyote. Of course, in spite of the fact they are matewames, they are not forced to eat Hikuri in great quantities; rather they have the option to take a lot, a little, or nothing.

POWER PLANTS VERSUS DRUGS

The relationship of the Wirrarika with peyote is something very unusual, which cannot be compared, nor is it in any way similar, to what peyote and other psychedelic plants represent to modern people. This has to do with the preparation they undergo during their lifetime, in which peyote has a deep religious significance, allowing the effects of the sacred cactus to constitute complete spiritual experiences.

For a city person, the experience with peyote is similar to their experience with other drugs in general—be it marijuana, hashish, LSD, hallucinogenic mushrooms, or any other. Their experience remains within the same hallucinogenic parameters in which they perceive distorted and chaotic images of the world they know. The Wirrarika, on the other hand, do not hallucinate nor are they submerged in chaos; rather they penetrate into the spiritual world which their elders have told them about since earliest infancy and toward which they are approaching little by little, by means of training their attention and perception.

A COLLECTIVE *DREAM*

Pedro de Haro told me the Wirrarika do not believe in their gods, but they perceive them directly. He was referring to the concrete fact that through different procedures, one of which is the ritual use of peyote, they are capable of penetrating a nonordinary reality, which the Wirrarika have sustained collectively throughout the centuries, and which they invariably maintain with a feeling of continuity. The gods and spirits the pilgrims see, and with whom they interact at Humun' Kulluaby, are the same ones maintaining the same attributes as those perceived by their Wirrarika ancestors centuries ago.

In Castanedian terms, we could say that Humun' Kulluaby, as a magic space located in the separate reality that corresponds to the desert zone called Humun' Kulluaby, is a collective *dream* the Wirrarika have been able to sustain (by *intending*[6] it) since time immemorial, thanks to persistently maintaining their rituals and spiritual practices generation after generation. On that side of reality, the Wirrarika do not become confused or scared. Rather they know what to do and within it they move with complete precision. Everything they

---

[6] See *The Art of Dreaming*, Carlos Castaneda, HarperCollins, New York, 1993.

perceive has a special significance—not only have they been able to move their *assemblage points*[7] to the precise position in which they can perceive the *separate reality* existent in Humun' Kulluaby, they can also fix them in that position. What's more, since they accomplish this procedure by means of a collective ritual in which their attention is aligned with that of their companions, the result is that everyone fixes their assemblage point on the same position and perceives the same separate reality in the same way as the Wirrarika of ancient generations.

Such a transformation in perception (movement of the assemblage point) does not rely on the consumption of peyote as its principal element. This is achieved, fundamentally, thanks to the specialized use of attention and of saving energy, generally obtained through various practices of abstinence—for example, fasting, celibacy, or avoiding anger. All of this produces the appropriate *intent*, and the ingesting of a small piece of peyote is no more than the "spark" that initiates the process, having an effect more symbolic than physical. Only the matewame or novice must consume abundant quantities of peyote, while the experienced jicarero requires very little or none, to the point where he or she can penetrate into the separate reality without consuming anything. On an everyday level, the *peyoteros* can be observed taking now and then a small quantity of Hikuri.

My personal experience, after my initial encounters with the Wirrarika, allowed me to discover that a minimum quantity of Hikuri—the size of an olive—does not produce hallucinations but rather great mental clarity and notable physical vigor, which makes it very appropriate for long journeys on foot. The same amount is also beneficial for many nonserious illnesses, such as colds and muscular aches.

---

[7] See *The Fire From Within*, Carlos Castaneda, Transworld Publishers, London, 1984.

THE TRUE KEY TO THE RITUAL

As far as rituals go, the consumption of a small portion of peyote is only one element that, by itself, will not superimpose nonordinary reality over ordinary reality. This requires many other factors such as the *offering to power*,[8] periods of fasting and abstinence, discipline, stopping the internal dialogue[9], dances, and so forth. Among other groups of Toltec descent, such as the Náhuas, where Hikuri is not present as a central element in their religion, it could be established that they attain similar states of perception without the use of any power plants.

The man in the city or the hippie who is quite asleep and lacking in available energy generally will not notice the effects of such a small portion of peyote and will have to consume several whole buttons to be able to "hallucinate," while obtaining ordinary, weakening, and on occasion, dangerous results.

We remain in the circle, which surrounds the offerings, long enough for the matewames to finish their bowls of peyote. Occasionally, the jicareros take a slice. Observing the matewames, I realize they are eating the bitter cactus, chewing it naturally without the slightest gesture of discomfort. They are all very young, between sixteen and twenty-two years approximately. Never will I forget the faces of some of my tewari matewame friends when they chewed their first slice of peyote! Although they had been forewarned as to the flavor, their expressions indicate they had never imagined its magnitude, and now they were finding out. Nevertheless, they do what they can to maintain serenity, and of course, they take much smaller portions than those taken by the Wirrarika. The fact is that without the experience of a life spent in similar rituals, they found themselves in difficult circumstances, with

---

[8] I refer to unusual efforts on behalf of life that are carried out in our own lives as a preparation for some important experience relative to the Spirit.

[9] See chapter VI of *The Teachings of Don Carlos*, Victor Sanchez, Santa Fe: Bear & Co., 1995.

far fewer means at their disposal than the jicareros to be able to deal with the Hikuri adequately. In any case, we were using all our recourses and experience in such areas of work as the handling of attention, stopping the internal dialogue, the awareness of the *other self*, and states of nonordinary reality, all obtained without the use of any drugs, as a counterweight to our condition as "novices" in the separate reality of the Wirrarika.

PARADISE ON EARTH

Even though I was relying on my varied experiences in nonordinary reality gained while living among the Wirrarika over several years, the Pilgrimage to Humun' Kulluaby constituted, without doubt, a much deeper and complex stage. The effects were evident not only in the elements of the ritual but also in the states of attention we were achieving with the passage of time. Partly it was the length of the Pilgrimage and all the rituals it involved, but mainly it was the very deep significance the Wirrarika attribute to Humun' Kulluaby—the paradise, the place that tells them of their destinies, the home of Tamatz Kahullumary, teacher of the marakames and one of the most important powers for every Wirrarika. From the beginning of the Pilgrimage I could perceive clearly the fear of the matewames who did not know what Humun' Kulluaby was, alongside the emotion and joy of the jicareros who had gone and who knew.

The entire Pilgrimage takes place, from its beginning in the sierra, in a state of nonordinary awareness and in a space that is not the space of the everyday world but rather that of the separate reality, where the world passes by in another way. At each moment, during the rituals or when we are moving from one point to another along the sacred route, we have visions of that *other world* in which Wirrarika were present. On occasion, we penetrate the *vision* and ourselves become magic beings congruent with that world. At other times, the vision speaks to us of our lives. Seen from this perspective, they reveal aspects that required a change or that would permit us a silent, profound, and exact understanding of matters that in everyday life are confusing. Many answers to questions that have been with us for a long time are given when we least expect them.

Most liberating is finding self in a state outside the ego and its demands for self-confirmation. Here in this desert among these men and women and in a moment such as this, history does not matter—neither the personal nor that of our respective societies. We are equal, one more mote of dust in the Mystery of the world. What wonder! What profound peace to forget the unreal self in which we live almost full time!

Once the matewames finish their bowls, we pick up our things and form a line to head back to camp. Each pilgrim returns with a voluminous load of peyote. The hunt has been successful. A good omen. The Pilgrimage is going well.

Surely the families of the jicareros, together in the Kalihuey of Santa Maria, who remain watchful and informed of everything occurring to the travelers by means of Grandfather Fire, will be feeling very content that everything is going well.

The long line of jicareros advances; it is already mid-afternoon and the fierce heat begins to diminish, giving way to a fresh breeze. The desert again transforms itself. Physically it has not changed, but the power that sustains it can be felt with strong clarity. In this place dwell many more things than meet the eye. Finally we arrive at camp where each one, without need of a single word, begins preparations for the night that approaches: the night of the Hikuri. Everyone knows exactly what to do.

THE SEAT OF TATEWARI

After taking care of their sacks of peyote and the rest of their things, the majority of the men go off to look for wood, since they must add to what they already have. When they return, they all bring sticks that are extraordinary: short, straight, and of the same size, without branches or protuberances. I realize that not just any piece of wood will serve to feed Tatewari. While they use any type of wood for cooking in the mountains so long as it burns, in the case of ritual fires, everything must meet special conditions, from the shape and size of the wood to how green or dry it is. Since Grandfather Fire is very old, this time he must be fed with green wood, less tough than old wood, making it easier for him to eat.[10]

The place where Tatewari will sit is prepared. A trunk is placed crosswise to serve him as a cushion. Then a series of trunks rest on the first one pointing to the place where the Sun rises. Only the urukuakame Luciano, the marakame Antonio (they being the eldest) or their direct assistants, Tamatz Kahullumary Manuel or Tatewari Julio, may light the fire. Antonio approaches the place where the seat of Tatewari has been prepared. He speaks of the Pilgrimage, of the great efforts made by all to reach Humun' Kulluaby. He asks that Tatewari accompany us and guard us throughout the night. He assures him, in exchange, that he will be cared for and fed as is his due, with his green wood and his pinole.[11]

Night falls on the group of pilgrims who, now and then, eat one more piece of peyote. There is no moon and the darkness is total, save for the light of Tatewari who warms and

---

[10] I can imagine what intelligent readers must be thinking: that old wood burns better than green wood but, incredible as it may seem, among the Wirrarika it happens the other way around. I've seen it myself. When I first began traveling with them, I saw them gathering green wood and in my arrogance, considering myself an "expert" in matters having to do with campfires, thought: "that wood is very green, it'll never catch." Much to my surprise, however, after placing a few small pieces of resinous wood underneath to help start the fire, the green wood flared up immediately, I would almost say exploded, because the flames suddenly became enormous. I failed to find an explanation for this, there being much more interesting things going on that begged for explanations. Once more I discovered that we, as city people, think we know everything, but oftentimes reality turns out to be very different from what we think.

[11] In Mexico, toasted corn flour, which is drunk by mixing it with hot or cold water.

protects us. All remain silent. The majority are seated with their arms crossed and heads bent over their knees, which are almost touching their chests. The jicareros begin their battle, they go in search of their vision; if they are lucky they will find themselves face-to-face with the Blue Deer.

THE SONG OF TATEWARI

I don't know what will happen, if there will be a dance or if the marakame will sing. There is nothing to indicate either way, so I recline underneath the mesquite with my head on my sleeping bag. I see the stars and I consider my life. My life! How distant my everyday life seems; although it is not an ordinary life, at times it is tiring. So much time coordinating groups, dictating conferences, or giving courses. So many people forming ideas about me, much closer to their fantasies than to my reality. How pleasurable that here nobody knows or cares about Victor Sanchez. Only the night knows truly who I am. I spy on her mystery, trying to get her to tell me. Useless. That type of answer doesn't exist in the mysterious.

It's a little cold. I move closer to Ligia and Luis Manuel, comforted in feeling their warmth although we are not touching. No one speaks. The Wirrarika seem asleep, although I see they are not. Where have they gone? They are far away! Later I hope I can catch up with them and know where they are, what it is they are doing.

I remember the fire. Although I am not looking, I clearly perceive its light and heat. I am about twelve meters from it, but its heat and light reach me without difficulty. Thanks. I realize what luck I've had in finding a teacher like that. The Wirrarika indeed know what they are doing. To learn, they do not search for human teachers, rather they convert themselves into apprentices of the sun! Of Grandfather Fire! The oldest, wisest, and strongest of the powers of the world. What master or guru can compete with such powers?

For a long time I don't think, I only feel and *see*. Without thoughts, without words, I see Tatewari sustaining the world with his power. I realize he is inside me as well, inside every-one. How is it possible that we live without perceiving the light that we are? The power that dwells in each one of us? We waste so much time searching for what has been inside all along. I understand why my Wirrarika brothers contemplate fire so much.

At a given moment, I realize I am singing. When did I begin? I feel it has been for some time now, although I did not use the control or the will I normally would use. This is the hour of the nagual and my ego is not in charge. What's more, it is not anywhere around here! I hear my song; it comes from I don't know where, but I like it very, very much. It is a song that speaks of Grandfather Fire, but I am not making it up. It is a gift of Tatewari that I can take with me, to sing when I am sad, or when for any reason I feel the need. The song floods my body. It floods everything, inside and out, like a tingling heat beginning in my chest and extending throughout my body. My mouth is not singing, nor my throat. I am singing with my entire energy field, and what's more, the one singing is not who I know as "I", but rather the energy of which I am composed! The "gift" continues for more than an hour. Thanks, Grandfather!

When the song finishes, I think for a moment. I was so deep into my experience that I did not consider the rest. Have I disturbed the Wirrarika? I turn around to look and I realize I have disturbed no one. They remain far away, traveling on the wings of perception. Next to the fire is René and one of the Wirrarika who is singing to the fire. I realize he is singing in Spanish. I try to hear what he is singing . . . He is singing "my" song! I don't know if he heard it from me or if Tatewari taught it to him as well, but I am very happy to hear it sung by a Wirrarika. Afterwards, silence again reigns.

"THE THING"

We have spent a long time sitting or reclining, and it makes us feel like getting up, stretching our legs, and walking a little. Originally, we had thought to follow to the letter the instructions they gave us to participate and imitate the ways of the Wirrarika. Nevertheless, now it is evident that each one has to go his own way and search for himself the path leading to his *vision* and then the way to the *encounter*. Antonio has told me, without opening his mouth, that we can go but to be careful and stay together. We'll see each other later.

The tewaris gather and after putting on our coats, we form a small line. We go into the desert walking very attentively. We use no flashlights. In these moments, the desert looks very different. In spite of not using flashlights and the lack of moonlight, our eyes adapt very well and we clearly perceive everything around us. The cacti and bushes are surrounded by a fine halo. We slowly advance down a path, but a shadow, which follows us, jumping on our right, causes us to accelerate our pace until we almost end up running. Not only can it be seen, it can be heard crushing the bushes each time it touches the ground. I am certain, in any case, we should not run or fall out of line. We stop about three hundred meters from the Wirrarika campsite in a small clearing of limestone sand. We turn around to confirm if everyone saw and heard the same. There is no doubt. Everyone saw it. We talk a little about the "thing" and decide that no one should remain by himself or walk alone. Not even to go to the bathroom.

The cold is very intense. We lay out some sleeping bags, one next to the other, tightly like a package of sausages. We cover our selves with jackets, sweaters, and a blanket that someone brought. There is a close feeling between us. What unites us is beyond conventional interests or agreements. What unites us are the battles we have waged together, and there have been many. What unites us is the privilege of having arrived at this point together.

VISIONS

We look at the sky and the show commences: a star that grows almost to the point of becoming a sun, shooting stars that last far longer than those we have known up till now. Later, Luis Manuel says:

"Did you see the wolf?"

"Wolf . . . ? Where?"

"Up there, in the sky!"

We turn to where he is pointing and sure enough, we see a wolf outlined in the sky; his eyes are two stars that shone with special brilliance. I get the shivers not from fear, but from emotion. Wolves and I have a lot in common. I continue with my friends, alternating moments of silence and visions that reveal to us aspects of the world we rarely notice, with moments in which our life comes to us, revealing itself in all its nakedness. Luis Manuel moves away about four meters. We think he should not be alone and so we call to him. He doesn't want to come, something that worries us. I get up and go over to him advising him, to return.

"Luisma, go back over there. What are you doing here alone?"

"Give me a chance, Vic, I have to be alone for a little while. I'm seeing something very important that I have been dragging around with me all my life, and I feel I have to stay here a little longer."

"But, are you sure you'll be all right?"

"Sure, I'll be right back."

I realize what is happening to him, and I join the others, who are already getting up to look for Luis Manuel. I stop them, telling them he is fine and that we should leave him alone for a moment.

After a while he returns and lays down by my side in the typical "sausage" position. I sense he is a little sad. In the sky an enormous shooting star traces its long trajectory before disappearing. I try to cheer him up:

"Did you see that shooting star, how enormous it was?"

"Yes, I saw it," he responds. I don't turn around to see, but I sense he is crying.

"Why are you sad? Didn't you see the shooting star?"

"Yes, I saw it, that's why I'm crying."

"But, why does it make you sad? Doesn't it seem beautiful to you?"

"Yes, it was very beautiful, but short-lived."

Suddenly I comprehend what is troubling him. I connect myself with his feeling and both of us begin to cry intensely. I have *seen* the loss of a very dear being, his irremediable disappearance and the love that remains, vibrating. I hug my friend, feeling his sadness to the core of my soul and trying to comfort him. We continue to cry for awhile, and Luis Manuel says:

"Now we are brothers, right, Vic?"

"Yes, Luisma, we are brothers!"

When we are able to stop crying, I tell him something I had just realized:

"Do you know something good about shooting stars?"

"What's that?"

"That in reality we shouldn't be so sad since, even if they are brief, the gift of their beauty and their light is great enough to make us happy for having received it, although only for an instant."

"That's right."

"But there's something still better."

"What's that?"

"What is better still is that when a shooting star goes out, in reality it hasn't gone out, it only has disappeared from our sight. Don't be so sad, Luisma, your star hasn't gone out, rather it's still shining there, in some part of this marvelous universe."

We continue for a while seeing the world and our lives. Each one wages his battle, which at times becomes very difficult. For myself, I feel very content since I see my path very clearly in front of me. Although it does not appear easy, it seems to me exciting and promising.

THE CARETAKER

"Did you hear that music?" asks Ligia, who is to my left.

"You're right! It's very beautiful." We continue listening a bit until I realize it seems to be someone singing.

"Who is singing?" I ask the group.

Since we are all lying down and covered up to protect us from the cold, nobody wants to get up to see where the music is coming from. An investigation begins: All members of the group are asked if they know who is singing. Each one has a different idea who it might be and we continue our speculations until everyone has denied having been the one singing.

"I know who is singing," says Ligia.

"Who?"

"It's Martín, the Wirrarika."

"Whooo . . . ?"

"Martín, who has come to take care of us."

I get up and look to my left; at the end of the package of sausages I see a Wirrarika sitting down and wrapped in a blanket. His face is buried in his arms, which rest on his knees. On his head is a baseball cap. Between the visor and the blanket, where he hides his face, through an opening can barely be seen his two eyes, which shine with intensity. Often Martín seems to be the most distracted of the Wirrarika. He understands Spanish, but he speaks no more than a few words. At that moment however, his look makes me realize he knows perfectly well what he is doing.

"Martín! What are you doing here?" I ask him and he doesn't respond. He merely smiles.

"He's watching over us," says Ligia. "He's been here for about half an hour watching over us with his songs. They sent him from the Wirrarika camp."

"Is that true, Martín?" Martín doesn't answer, he merely smiles again.

THE SEARCH FOR FIRE

We continue with our visions, silence returns, and Martín disappears in the same way as he appeared, without our realizing it. An hour passes and suddenly René says:

"Hey, now I know why we're all sad!"

"Why?" everyone asks.

"Because we're far from Tatewari."

"The Grandfather Fire! It's true! We have to go for firewood and light a fire. Who wants to look for firewood?"

Silence in the night. With that "thing" jumping about in the brush, nobody wants to go.

"I'll go with whoever will go with me," I tell everyone.

"I'll go with you," says René.

"Me too," says Manolo.

"Well, let's go!"

We form a "mini Indian file" and steer ourselves toward the Wirrarika. On the way, the jumping shadow returns to hound us again, this time on our left, only now it comes much closer. I can even hear it squeaking. We feel the need to get to where the fire is so we quicken our pace. I feel some relief when we see the silhouette of the university truck. At last we arrive at the Wirrarika camp.

They are spread out on the ground, wrapped in blankets. It is clear they are not asleep. Entering the Wirrarika camp is like penetrating a "sphere of attention," within which everything is under perfect control. We find Tayau and another Wirrarika standing next to the fire. We ask him if we can take some wood for our fire and we tell him about the "thing that jumps" among the bushes.

"Uuuhh, sure why not! Yes it's very dangerous to go out there without the protection of Tatewari. It surprises me that you're still in one piece!"

(Gulp!) "Then we can take the wood?"

"Sure man, but hurry! Don't leave the others alone!"

We gather the wood and leave once more, this time ready to avoid turning around or paying attention to the "thing." We pass among the bushes trying to appear at ease, but involuntarily our legs begin to walk faster as the thing becomes more aggressive. Instinctively, we grab a piece of wood to "arm" ourselves in case of attack. Without realizing how, we end up running at full speed until we reach our friends.

We light a small fire, following Wirrarika methods the best we can. The fire comforts us, but does not seem sufficient to lessen the cold, which becomes more intense. To counteract it we return to the "package of sausages" position, and cover ourselves as best we can. We hear the nocturnal sounds of the desert, which take us traveling among its brush. The desert is alive even to its last recesses.

THE MEN OF FIRE

The wind begins to pick up and we cover our faces as well, since our noses threaten to freeze. After a time, I hear Manolo's voice calling me from somewhere outside the package.

"Hey, Vic, come and see this!" I poke my face out of the blanket and manage to see Manolo, looking at the bushes with amazement.

"What are you looking at? Come back here!"

"No, Vic. You have to see this, you won't regret it."

My curiosity vanquishes the cold. I get up and stand next to him. I look in the direction he is looking, which is toward the Wirrarika camp. I see a small light among the bushes, which suddenly increases in size until it fills the entire scene in front of our eyes.

"Son of a gun, this isn't possible! Come here quick and see!" I tell the rest who are still lying on the ground.

"What's going on?" several ask. They subsequently get on their feet and make exclamations of amazement. We can't believe what we are seeing.

The vision in front of our eyes is of the Wirrarika campfire, which in fact was outside our field of vision due to the distance and the height of the bushes in the area. We see some Wirrarika seated around the campfire, immersed in something having to do with it exclusively. But the view we have of them is in no way normal; they are made of multicolored light as though they are a ball of fire "hidden" under a hat and blanket. They are made of the same material as Tatewari and they know it. Suddenly they seem to notice that we are observing them, and two of them turn to look at us. We feel fear like a sudden slap. Their eyes are of fire and they are focused toward us. They manage a slight smile and turn to watch the fire. We remain in ecstasy for some minutes.

Then we see the flames of the fire grow until they are transformed into an enormous deer face with large antlers of fire. He looks directly at us with flames flaring from his eyes and mouth. We are rubbing our eyes as if trying to wake up. What we see is real! That is Tamatz Kahullumary there in front of us! All six of us see him! That enormous flaming deer face among the Wirrarika is the most exquisite vision we have ever had. It is emanating the power and majesty of another world. Tears of happiness run from my eyes. We are all expressing our amazement and delight with expressions such as: "It's not possible that something so beautiful exists! I can't believe it! How wonderful! Are you seeing it? Do you see it too?" The vision continues for about fifteen minutes.

A little later the Deer of Fire is "absorbed" by the blaze and once more we are looking at the luminous Wirrarika. Some are standing and two are seated next to the fire. The impression they give of being made of fire is not only visual, rather I can sense bodily the tremendous energy under the hats, the clothes, and the blankets that contain them. It is as though at any moment their clothes are going to ignite and they will be converted into plain fire. The figure seated to the right is doing something we cannot discern. He is bending rhythmically toward the fire. Soon everything is made clear.

He is talking to the fire. It is the marakame Antonio talking to the fire! The fire answers him. It is plain that they understand one another perfectly. They are of the same nature. As the marakame continues to communicate with the fire, the other figures spread themselves out and become smaller as though they are preparing to fly. The intensity of interaction between both increases. The profound love that the Wirrarika and particularly Antonio has for the fire can be felt. Only in that moment Antonio is not simply Antonio. He is pure energy. Also there can be felt an inexpressible and infinite love from Grandfather Fire for the Wirrarika. They are without doubt his nation, his people. They are perhaps the only ones awake on the Earth, and now they are letting us spy on their world for just a moment. I realize the titanic task the Wirrarika carry on their shoulders, sustaining for centuries and millennia an unbending effort to not forget the essential, to keep open the channels connecting with the source of everything existing.

THE LIGHT OF THE WORLD

The figures around the fire begin to rise, radiating an intense red-yellow light like fire. They stop about fifty centimeters above the ground without taking their eyes off Tatewari, with whom they are in full communication. They look like suns outlined against the infinite darkness of the universe. The effort of the marakame increases. He is calling upon Tatewari to enter into him, giving him his force and his power. A thick line of liquid fire stretches out from the flames until it touches the marakame at the height of his abdomen, his shape grows and from him an immense light begins to radiate. He is illuminating the world! The emotion is so great, I cannot stop crying and laughing. Finally I understand it! I finally end up understanding the mission of the marakames on the Earth: to illuminate the world! That old legend of the warriors who merged in the task of the Sun was not just a metaphor after all. It was there in front of my own eyes. I give thanks with all my being to the Spirit for not having abandoned us on the Earth. I give thanks that there exist beings like these to remind us of our true nature—we are luminous beings, little suns! I give thanks, and as I do, I promise to fight with all my being in order to not forget. To not forget and to live accordingly.

Other things take place that night, but the vision—which was a gift from Antonio to us—is so strong and revealing, it fills me up so much, that with it I prefer to close my tale of that night.[12]

THE OFFERINGS OF LA' UNARRE

The next day we wake with the sunshine falling brightly on the world. We had slept a little toward dawn and now it is around nine in the morning. All the feelings we had seen and experienced are there, present in our bodies. We are not completely in right-side awareness. We, nevertheless, have to yield to the new day and what it brings, all of us choosing not to talk about what had occurred, instead concentrating on our tasks. I don't know whether the Pilgrimage is already over, but instinctively I opt to organize my things and prepare the vehicles for getting underway, although I have not the slightest desire to return to the "civilized" world. We are a little tired but ready for what will follow. At this point, having hardly slept or eaten seems natural to us, appropriate for the work we are doing.

Internally, I ask myself about what I have experienced in Humun' Kulluaby, and in particular about the previous evening. Was I remembering all that had taken place? Were the implications of those visions on my life clear? My sensation is that one part of me knows and understands, while the rational side feels confused. I choose not to force myself and I am confident that in time each piece would find its place. I see that some Wirrarika remain where they were, while others

---

[12] In the face of that sublime vision, there also appeared the stupidity of man in all its crude magnitude. How much pettiness! What useless waste to live pursuing empty aims when our nature is the same as that of the Sun! To be suns, yet to live in filth! What stupidity!!

pack up assorted articles and make ready to depart. I decide to ask.

"What's next, Antonio?"

"La' Unarre!"

"The La' Unarre?"

"Yes, Victor, we're going to La' Unarre," responds the marakame as he turns to busy himself with his bag, in which he packs assorted objects. I approach Tayau to ask him for more details.

"Hey, Tayau, are you ready to go to La' Unarre?"

"Not at all, only the fat heads go there!"

"What do you mean only the fat heads, doesn't everyone go?"

"Of course not, only the principal ones go: the marakame, the urukuakame, Tamatz Kahullumary, Julio and whoever else Antonio decides upon; he's in charge."

"And why doesn't everyone go?"

"There is no need, the way is very difficult, but those who climb the Mountain carry everyone's offerings with them, to thank God that everything turned out well in the Pilgrimage, and so that He knows that all the Wirrarika will continue to remember. It is a very important place; there was born Tamatz Kahullumary, later he came down from the mountain and ran to this place, Humun' Kulluaby, and from his footprints sprang roses (peyote),[10] that's why it's a very important place."

I turn around to look toward one edge of the desert at the mountains, which look so far away, and I try to locate La' Unarre. Sure enough there it is, the highest peak of them all. It seems like a long way to go to get there, and I calculate that even using the truck or the cars, we will take many hours to arrive.

---

[10] Although among the Wirrarika of Santa Maria I have not often heard of peyote referred to as roses or little roses, the allegory was familiar to me since I had heard it among those of other communities on frequent occasions.

After Tayau's explanation, it is obvious to me that the tewaris will not climb La' Unarre since we have no "fat heads" among us. At any rate, I am ready to take the pilgrims to the skirts of the mountain, and help them in any way I can.

I tell my companions what will happen. We decide to prepare our offerings, just in case, and everyone opts to accompany the "principal" Wirrarika to the skirts of the Mountain. This would permit us to make some light repairs to the cars, and if we're lucky, even change the oil—how badly they need it—while we are waiting the return from the Sacred Mountain, to then take them back to where the rest of the pilgrims are waiting. Other Wirrarika who will not climb the mountain also board the truck; they want to take advantage of the fact that we will be passing through "Los Valdés"[11] so they can purchase some things.

I ride in the back part of the truck. I have an enormous curiosity to know anything my teokari Wirrarika might say about the previous evening, and I go hoping to be able to discuss it with them. They are happy as always. We travel standing up, tying down our hats to keep them from flying away in the wind. I ask some how it went and they answer that it went very well, they saw and knew many things, but they seem little inclined to discuss the content of their visions. I respect their attitude and we end up talking of other things.

The mountains in the background approach gradually, while the truck advances rocking over the irregular terrain. I am clearly aware of the contrast between the feeling of camaraderie and fluid communication, which we share now, and the initial disquiet that both Wirrarika and tewaris had in the beginning. In spite of the fact I was aquainted with about half of the pilgrims, especially the "principal," it is very different

---

[11] a little town in the desert

to find myself with the full group of jicareros, some with their families and others who joined at the last minute. In addition, this is the first year of the five years the jicareros had to fulfill their responsibility and, therefore, their first Pilgrimage together, which made their initial nervousness a little greater. Now, however, the point and principal objective of the Pilgrimage was completed and everyone is much more relaxed.

As we get closer, the configuration of the mountains seems more surprising; the desert is completely flat and at its edge there suddenly appear very high mountains, without any intervening slope or incline whatsoever. At least that is the impression they give from this distance. Although I have been at the Mountain on other occasions, I realize the initial ascent will be very different on this side. Here the climb is straight from the desert floor to the summit. The usual ascent near Real de Catorce, at an altitude quite near the summit, can be approached by car or bus and from there, walked the rest of the way up to the point of the Palace.

We arrive at Los Valdés, a town typical of the Potosinian desert, although quite a bit larger than the settlements we've run across until now. We ply its dusty streets until we find a store where we can buy some refreshments; at this point we will have to separate ourselves temporarily. The two automobiles will remain here for maintenance, and the truck, together with those in charge of carrying the offerings, will continue on its way to where the ascent will begin, for the Sacred Mountain is still far off.

We begin to organize ourselves over the tasks we will carry out once back in town and agree with Antonio's group as to what time and where we will meet again. At that moment one of the Wirrarika informs me that we should send one or two of our group to carry our offerings in representation of the rest. This is a great surprise. There are two places available. Immediately we hold a separate meeting to evaluate who would be the most likely candidates to climb La' Unarre with the Wirrarika. Everyone wants to go. There follow several different opinions, then Manolo says: "The truth is, I really want to go, but I have climbed it before, therefore, I yield my place to someone who is not familiar with the sacred site." I recognize his gesture of solidarity and decide to second it: Let those go who have not gone before, the rest of us will stay behind to wash the cars and change the oil.

There are three who have not gone before, and they prepare themselves hoping it will not be inconvenient that three are going instead of two. We hand them our offerings and we give them a message for the powers that inhabit the high regions above. When everything is ready, I approach Antonio to explain who will be our representatives and to ask about the time and place we can meet when they come down off the Mountain. "You have to go, Victor," he tells me quietly while he looks at me with eyes that leave no room for any other consideration. In that moment I experience a sudden change of attention.

Only an instant before Antonio's words, my attention was the everyday attention of the right side. After receiving the order, something in me changes, and I find myself perceiving the world with an alertness that is out of the ordinary. I can feel the vibrant atmosphere in my entire body. I experience an extraordinary and silent mental clarity, and my relation with the world is much more intense. It is like being able to feel anything upon which I focus my attention. I turn toward the mountains and I clearly feel the call. Antonio is right. I have to go to the Palace of the Governor: the Sun. There is nothing more to say. I explain to Manolo I have to go by order of the marakame. In a few minutes, those of us in charge of carrying out the task are up in the university truck, headed for La' Unarre.

After about half an hour, we arrive at a small village, located at the foot of the Sacred Mountain. Everything is ready to begin the hike. We say good-bye to Ventura and agree to meet him at four (at four? but it's almost eleven in the morning!). I keep my thoughts to myself and I prepare myself for the task. As it stands, seven Wirrarika and four Mexicans will go. We form an indian file and begin to walk at a good pace. In spite of the fact that I have walked and climbed mountains for many years, the pace of these Wirrarika demands that I concentrate to the maximum.

The music of the violin and the guitar completes the perfect atmosphere for the climb. Galindo, who plays the small guitar, is at the end of the line. Ahead of me goes Julio playing his violin. I have observed in all the dances of the jicareros, it is always Julio who places himself at the head of the line of dancers, while giving indications for the changes of direction or the dance form as well. Ahead of Julio goes Antonio, ahead of him, his venerable Tamatz Kahullumary (Manuel); and, heading the line, the urukuakame Luciano, the eldest of all.

Very focused, I move forward and then I "disappear." The perception of my "self" vanishes, and soon I become part of a much greater field of energy. It is as though I am but one part of the energy field created by all of us who are walking in the line. The sensation of forming a part of "this thing" that is moving and advancing is very intense and pleasurable. We move forward a few kilometers, shortening the distance between the village and the mountain. We stop for a few moments while some of us "go to the bathroom." I contemplate the Sacred Mountain, now from its base. It looks imposing. An enormous chasm opens a little beyond where we are, and climbs in a pronounced slope that appears straight up and down all the way to the summit. A great emotion floods me, contemplating the approaching challenge. I feel something very important is waiting for me up there; moreover, I feel a kind of internal urgency to climb up and meet it.

"Go in front of me, you are also urukuakame."

The voice of Julio brings me out of my observations of the Mountain. Although I understand the significance of the word urukuakame (he who indicates the way), I am not sure what he is referring to. I obey him without thinking and fall in just behind Antonio, which pleases me. I get ready to follow his pace, to step precisely in the place where he steps. We begin walking again and suddenly I hear behind me a melody that is at once familiar: it is the song Tatewari taught me in Humun' Kulluaby. Julio is singing some verses of "my" song! In Spanish! I feel very happy he likes my song from Tatewari, although I cannot understand how he learned it if I sang it only once. For a while we sing together, while we cover the distance separating us from the Mountain.

We enter the chasm and begin to climb. The slope is quite pronounced but, far from feeling tired, my body makes the necessary adjustments and pushes forward. Our pace is agile and rhythmic. In actuality it is Luciano setting the pace. At his seventy some years, he moves up the Mountain as though he were a mountain goat, taking long agile strides, and leaping from one side to the other each time a fissure blocks our way. On occasion, his jumps are so long, or the paths he takes are so complicated, that I have the impression he is testing us to see if we are equal to it. Antonio is also older than seventy years, but nevertheless, he moves much better in his sandals than I with my all-terrain boots.

The climb is really quite demanding for everyone. Two of my friends begin to fall behind. We go on ahead, and I have hope they will be able to catch up. Two Wirrarika come behind me, after them comes Luis Manuel, perfectly integrated with the rhythm of walking. When the way becomes more difficult, I can hear Antonio exclaim: "Oh my God! Oh my God!" to which everyone reacts with laughter and jokes without slackening our pace in the least. We continue at a rapid pace, and now and then we hear Antonio: "Oh my God, I'm too old for this! Poor me!" His playful tone is obvious. Attitudes such as this reflect very clearly the Wirrarika way of facing effort with a light tone, without ever entering into self-importance. It is plain that Antonio's clowning is intended more to lighten the work of the others than his own. He is going so well that on top of the effort of climbing the demanding mountain at a good pace, he still gives himself the luxury of clowning around, speaking and laughing for the joy of others.

The climb continues in this joyful tone, except for my two friends who have not managed to catch up. After a couple of hours, we pause at an enormous fissure in the chasm. We walk along it and arrive at a point where a thread of water runs over the ground. We stop there and drink the fresh water coming from the interior of the Mountain. It really is refreshing, and drinking it we feel how its energy reconstitutes us and fills us with strength. I move over to a small cave covered by rocks. I remove one of the rocks and shine a small flashlight inside to spy out its interior. I realize the water originates from here, and I remember the sacred value the Wirrarika give to the water holes there in Humun' Kulluaby.

Antonio gives me a sign to continue removing the rocks, and I begin to open the entrance to the cave. When the opening is wide enough, I crawl in and I realize it is a place of veneration. Many Wirrarika offerings are found in the interior of the cave. I greet the Spirit that inhabits this place and respectfully leave an offering. I come out as the marakame approaches the entrance and begins his invocations to the powers of the place. He waves his muvieri, "opening" the door to the sacred enclosure. Each one of the Wirrarika leaves an offering to the goddess of the place, relative of Tatei Matinieri. Later, Antonio draws water from the cave with a small cup. With his muvieri he scatters water on each one of us, while showering us with blessings, which we receive with joy and emotion. My two friends who had fallen behind arrive at last and in time to receive the blessings.

I am seated on a rock, next to the entrance of the cave, with the sun engulfing me, my body wet with the sacred water maintaining an agreeable sensation of freshness. The place is very beautiful, the moment perfect, and the company incomparable. In this state I find myself, when I feel a slight push on my left shoulder. I turn around and see Tamatz Kahullumary-Manuel handing me a muvieri. It is a small arrow, with yarn and eagle feathers, which are highly regarded by the Wirrarika. Except for the marakames who carry them in a case made of palm leaves, they customarily carry one or more on their hats. Each one is earned only as a result of a battle of power, some very special event, or some extraordinary event in favor of the Spirit. Often I have heard of the muvieri carried on the hat referred to as "the Spirit."

Many times I had observed with interest the muvieri of the Wirrarika, but I never had the absurd notion of "fabricating" one for myself or even thought of trying to buy or ask for one. Nevertheless, in this moment, to receive a muvieri from the hands of none other than Tamatz Kahullumary himself was something I deeply valued. Once I received it, I followed Manuel's instructions and fixed it to my hat. I put the hat on again and realized it felt very different. It was as if charged with something else. From now on, putting my hat on would possess a greater significance. I knew I would use it only on my outings in Wirrarika territory, or on very special occasions.

Invigorated by our stay at the water hole, we return to our path toward the summit. The way now becomes steeper. I observe that the younger Wirrarika have more difficulty on the ascent than the older ones. It's not that they do it badly; rather what occurs among the Wirrarika most deeply involved in spiritual matters, as the oldest ones are likely to be, is that not only are they the wisest, they are also the strongest and most vigorous. At this moment, Luciano and Antonio are setting a pace the younger ones can barely maintain. I follow close behind Antonio, marveling to see how he moves in the mountains. As we advance, he seems to get stronger.

The column halts once more to wait for my two friends who continue to fall behind. I look to see how far we have to go and I realize it will be the most difficult. I turn around to look at Antonio who remains silent. I know with certainty that under no circumstances should we arrive separately at the summit of the Mountain. When my friends finally arrive, I ask them if they can withstand the pace or would it be better if they wait for us at the bottom. They look toward the summit and decide to turn back. I lament their turning back, but I feel it is the most appropriate decision. They give us their offerings and begin to descend, while we turn to continue the ascent. Something amazing happens.

As if we had got rid of a heavy weight, we begin to walk with great lightness. In spite of the fact the climb is very steep with no place to rest, I feel as if we had wings on our feet; an internal force pushes us to climb, making us feel stupendous. Antonio stops and tells me, indicating a mountain to our right: "Did you see the train? How beautiful!" Everyone laughs and agrees that it is very beautiful. I don't see the train, but I feel they are referring to something more than a joke. We continue climbing; I see the old ones ahead of me and I recall how many days they have gone practically without sleeping or eating. I begin to think of the long trips they must make throughout the year before coming here: Rapavillame (Chapala, Jalisco), Aramara (San Blas), and Aurramanaka (Durango) among others. In each place there are rituals, long hikes, nights in vigilance, long fasts. I think of the frequent evenings Antonio spends as a singer, singing on occasion for three days straight. I think of what we have covered and how much is left to do until the Pilgrimage cycle is finished.

I see the material poverty of this powerful man walking in front of me and I understand truly what it means to live free from the yoke of self-importance. There is no rest in the life of the marakame; he never receives payment for his work, in money or in kind. On the contrary, all of his duties as marakame imply expenditures for which no one helps him. So why does he do it? What is his interest? The Spirit, not material rewards, not the ego. Looking at these beings with their lives dedicated to serve, carrying on their shoulders the enormous responsibility to prevent the rest of humankind from forgetting everything, to keep open the ways that carry us to the Spirit, I feel happy to witness the incredible—there are Men of Knowledge! It is possible to vanquish self-importance!

That old ragged man there, in front of me, is without a doubt much more imposing and much finer than those sorcerers and "perfect" masters about whom the books and stories, which deal with superhuman guides and their apprentices chosen by power, have spoken. Here we are, people of flesh and blood! No one told me, I didn't read it anywhere, I am living it! I wouldn't change a fraction of what I have lived here for the most extraordinary fantasies that books or narrated stories could offer me. My choice has been appropriate. To live for myself. To undertake with enthusiasm and joy that which I can conquer on my own two feet, with my own body. This is the magic of truth! Its value is infinitely higher than the sum of all the exotic and spectacular books I can read about the Spirit. For sure, Antonio is not perfect, but he is full of that which we badly need to recover, the possibility of living in accordance with the Spirit. Best of all, I can shake his hand! I am seeing him and we are here, in the place where dwells Tamatzin!

We keep climbing and I begin to realize the true meaning of ascending La' Unarre. During this ascent, everything I've lived and learned during the Pilgrimage begins to "fall into place" and finds meaning in my inner self. I continue to climb and many revelations come to me. Finally I have found the place long sought for—a search begun with questions and doubts, then passed through schools and books that spoke of knowledge. Inside me, accepting my presence in this world, was the place we erroneously look for outside ourselves. At the end, the most elemental, and maybe the first thing I discovered, proved to be true—everything begins and ends inside oneself. The path is toward the inner; there lies the true master. What keeps us from it is nothing more than the worship of our own ego, which at times we disguise as the worship of someone or something else—be it a person we profess to be in love with, a mental fantasy about knowledge to which we are tied, or a search for freedom through the presence of some "perfect master." Waiting for them to teach us is, after all, the best excuse for not learning by ourselves.

What enormous power this mountain has! I feel its energy inside me; it enters through my feet and allows me to see. My eyes clear, allowing me to see and know what I have been lacking. I feel complete. I understand why the Wirrarika have such veneration for this place. Here is where it starts. This is the beacon that illuminates the magic world of the Wirrarika. Here is the guide, the answer. This is why they refer to the Blue Deer—who was born here—as a Master who teaches the correct way to live. Everything acquires meaning and each piece falls into place. In effect, the ascent of La' Unarre is a key element. It is the external expression and the catalyst that pro-vokes an "ascent" within ourselves. When we began to climb the mountain we were just people, but on the way we were transformed and now, near the summit, we are converted into sacred beings.

The summit is closer. As we draw near, my excitement increases. What's more, something else is waiting for me up there, and I'm going for it. When we arrive at the summit, we are full of power, transformed into magic beings who, as such, naturally inhabit a magic world. We are in the source of everything, THE CENTER OF THE WORLD!! Here is where everything began! Where everything keeps on beginning! What absolute joy. At last I have discovered it!

THE PROMISE FULFILLED

We head directly for the left side of the mountain, the side of the Wirrarika. We arrive at the area of the offerings and Antonio greets the powers that reside there. He blesses each one of us and all that we carry with us with his muvieri, thus reinforcing the state of grace in which we find ourselves. He speaks to Tamatz and tells Him of all that we have struggled, of all that we have fought to arrive to Him. Antonio weeps as he speaks with the Blue Deer, and we all weep while we feel his presence. Everything has meaning. Everything. Everything Antonio does, everything the others do, everything I do. Suddenly, a shot of awareness makes me reel. There comes to me the memory of that forgotten episode long ago, which happened to me on this same mountain. I was standing on the right side. I saw a line of Wirrarika who, in a state of high concentration, had climbed the mountain and passed in front of me. A feeling touched the core of my soul then: How I would like to be there inside, participating and understanding what was taking place!

The promise had been fulfilled!! Here I was, in the midst of the jicareros from Santa Maria, participating, seeing, and understanding everything! Laughter and tears were joined together in me. Thus I would discover to what extent we are related to everything existing, to what extent the Spirit listens when we ask from the core of our soul and are capable of backing up our dreams with powerful and decisive acts. Thank you, La' Unarre! Thank you, Tamatz Kahullumary! Thank you, Humun' Kulluaby! Thank you, Antonio and the teokaris jicareros! The endeavor does not end here. Rather, it has barely begun.

I look at Luis Manuel and I realize that for him there are also tremendous things happening. We embrace, happy to have arrived together at this place, beyond the borders of ordinary reality. Definitely we are brothers.

Full of feeling, we begin to place the offerings. The Wirrarika advise us to hide them well, to keep the mestizos from stealing them. Among the offerings of the Wirrarika are the beautiful deer antlers, which had been placed before on the altars set up in each one of the sacred places during the Pilgrimage. I have observed that these antlers are very highly valued by the Wirrarika, not only for having belonged to the animal they love most, but also because that particular animal surrendered to them during a ritual hunt, as that is the only way to obtain something so valuable. To leave an offering like that is an act of true generosity that reveals the effort implied by the offering. Among the antlers offered are included the most beautiful and largest of all, which are covered by a fine golden fur.

We place our offerings, while we speak to the Power of La' Unarre, explaining what the offering means to us and asking him to welcome it in his bosom. A tie stronger than time and space is established with this place. I know I will return here with my dreaming body and with my physical body. I know I will return here in my last flight just before the instant of my death. Now it is very clear why we saw—in that experience in Humun' Kulluaby without the Wirrarikas—rays of light emanating from the Sacred Mountain. La' Unarre is that—a beacon in the darkness, amidst the mysterious. Its light would now accompany me for all my existence, and that was something which nothing or no one would ever be able to change.

GATE OF POWER IN LA' UNARRE

Once we have delivered the offerings, we prepare to leave. We all express at once, aloud, our profound gratitude to the place. For the last time we contemplate the beauty of the world as seen from La' Unarre. I make the gesture of capturing between my hands the feeling this moment and place instill within me, then draw them to my chest. We form an indian file and begin our descent. The old ones again demand the maximum from the rest of us, since this time they do not descend at a fast walk, rather they take off at an all-out run down the steepest part of the mountain. It is a true march of power over slippery sand, loose rocks, nopal, and thorny cactus. This time there is no rest; once we began we would not stop running until we arrived at the base of the mountain.

A short while after beginning our descent, I feel as if my ears are adapting themselves to an abrupt change of pressure, and I hear something coming "uncorked" inside me. A state of heightened awareness allows me to put myself inside that tunnel of energy opened by those who go ahead of me. I remain in my place, behind Antonio. This time there is no music, since the musicians need to apply themselves to the maximum to withstand the pace of the old ones. We need total concentration—if I hesitate for an instant, I run into thorns or hit a rock. Don't think, don't think, just flow, let yourself go full of life and power.

We continue to descend very rapidly, then a voice, which is not my thought, begins to speak to me. It begins to give me a complicated and detailed explanation about the era in which we live and the task which I have to perform. I receive a long series of instructions about what I must and must not do in the next stage of my work. All the doubts I had in relation to what I should or should not write in my next book found a convincing answer—the voice is dictating it to me line by line with perfect wording. There is not one word that can be changed. I continue my descent and the dictating continues as well at great speed. I listen, trying not to miss details, knowing the task of remembering what I am receiving will be a long and arduous struggle.[1] My mental effort in trying not to lose a single word the voice is telling me begins to fatigue me; there comes a moment when it even becomes painful. A part of me wants the voice to be still. But deep inside I know the time remaining for listening to the voice is not very long, therefore, I have to make the effort and try to make use of each instant. Not even by relying on a tape recorder could I register even a small part of everything that is said to me, such is the speed with which the voice expresses its message. Paradoxically, it is perfectly clear.

I arrive at the flat area on the skirts of the mountain, exhausted not so much due to physical effort, but because of the mental effort required to retain the details of what the voice has told me. My body feels stupendous, alive to its

---

[1] Even though I have put my best effort into waging this battle, I have to admit that, in trying to represent in the present text all that I received during that gait of power, I have not achieved it, not even an approximation.

uttermost recesses. Once down on flat territory, the all-out run gives way to a rhythmic walk at a good pace. It is getting dark. My watch says 7:10 p.m. We find Ventura leaning up against the truck and drinking soda pop, next to a small store. Our friends, the two tewaris who had turned back at the middle, have not arrived yet. I honk the horn of the truck thinking that if they are lost, they can't be far away. They do in fact arrive a few minutes later and tell us that after getting lost and much walking, they arrived at the town from the other side, in such a way that their arrival almost coincided with ours. There are refreshments for everyone, and then everyone is on the truck. We return in darkness without a word until we arrived at Los Valdés.

After investigating a little we find our friends. We know where they are since we find the two cars parked on a street, absolutely shining, without a speck of dust. They don't seem like the same cars that had gone into the desert down such winding roads. My friends shine brightly as well—bathed and combed. It was then that I realize we are really a dirty mess, but happy. After greeting them with gladness, we are given some sandwiches they had prepared for everyone. We decide to rest briefly and enjoy the sandwiches before continuing on our way to the Wirrarika camp, well inside the desert. Antonio and the rest of the Wirrarika want to go on immediately since they know their families and the other jicareros will be anxious. That's fine, we'll catch up soon; after all, the cars are faster than the truck.

Only the tewaris remain eating sandwiches and talking about the incidents of the day. I do not feel ready to talk about everything that occurred coming down from La' Unarre. I only manage to tell them: The climb to the Palace is not merely a stage. In some way, it provides the key that allows total understanding of what the Pilgrimage is all about.

RETURN TO THE MOUNTAINS

After desperately turning around in the desert for about two hours, we decide to return to the way that leads out of the town. We are completely lost in an interminable labyrinth of "paths" without any point of reference to orient ourselves in this darkness that is like the mouth of a wolf. We keep trying time and again, until I begin to fear we will run out of gas, far from anywhere. Only the distant lights of Los Valdés provide the sole point of contact we have for a possible exit. My hope is that, when they see we haven't arrived, maybe the Wirrarika will come back to look for us. In the last instance we can spend the night there, having a much better opportunity to find them during the day.

An hour and a half later, we hear the sound of the truck. Ventura is there with all the Wirrarika. The nonstop return journey to the sierra has begun.

> Humun' Kulluaby, Humun' Kulluaby,
> who knows why
> the roses cry.[2]
>
> Who could say why?
> Who could guess why?
> Humun' Kulluaby, Humun' Kulluaby,
> who knows why
> the roses cry.[3]

---

[2] Roses or little roses, the affectionate name the Wirrarikas give to peyote.

[3] Indigenous song. Taken from a compilation by Fernando Benitez, volume II of *Los Indios de Mexico*, Era publisher.

ABOUT THE AUTHOR

After the wonder of his first encounters with indigenous peoples, Victor Sanchez set out to study academic anthropology. From there he returned to the indigenous world and discovered "anti-anthropology," an attitude of investigation that places emphasis on the human experience in the encounter with the *otherness*, not on intellectual reports that reduce reality to the narrow limits of a theoretical framework.

Although he is a young man, he has over seventeen years experience in different fields that together have caused him to bring forth a teaching on personal growth called "The Art of Living Purposefully."

From his adventures in the world of nature (crossing deserts, jungles, and mountains, or exploring communication with whales and dolphins) he sees the reencounter with that world as the ideal space within which to reencounter our natural self and find the answers to our fundamental questions. In his work, this encounter with nature is not an intellectual approximation or an ecology of the mind. It is participation of the body and an ecology that comes from the heart and is expressed through a way of living.

From his experience with indigenous groups in Mexico—survivors who keep alive the spiritual traditions of the ancient Toltecs—he brings us a message: We are children of the Sun, our nature is to shine and, as double beings, we must reincorporate into our daily lives the awareness of the *other self* that lies hidden inside us, waiting to be resurrected in order to show us the Toltec we all unknowingly carry within.

Inspired by the books of Carlos Castaneda, Victor Sanchez developed a wide variety of techniques and a methodology for personal growth and spiritual development like no one has ever done before him. He has grounded the restlessness of millions of readers who, though profoundly interested in the works of Castaneda, could not find in these works the elements and clarity that would permit them to connect the unusual adventures that are described with their own daily experiences as city people. Thanks to the practical tools developed by Victor Sanchez, these readers no longer have to confine their interest in Castaneda's work to imagination, fantasy, or to a nostalgia of the impossible. Now they can transform this interest into a practical experience applicable to their own world and to the progressive enrichment of their everyday life.

The proposals of Victor Sanchez are not mere affirmations whose existence terminates with the pages of a book or in the realm of thoughts; rather they are an open invitation to the practices that can incorporate them as a living substance into our daily experience. The workshops and seminars he has given through the years express clearly that his message is not directed to the sphere of thinking; rather, it points to the realm of experiences.

Above all, his work is an invitation for us to get away from thinking and talking about knowledge, and instead, to begin to live it in our body and our heart, within the context of our everyday life and people. It is an invitation to take our own responsibility rather than to go on waiting for someone else to take it for us. And this is because what we are searching for—as the author says—is inside us. The only prerequisite is to recover the essential experience of listening to ourselves, penetrating to that inner space where the Spirit dwells, from where it speaks to us without words, through what the author calls Silent Knowledge.

In *The Teachings of Don Carlos*, the author relates the testimony of his experience in developing and applying a practical methodology inspired by the books of Castaneda, and whose development was brought about through the means given to him from his experience among the indigenous peoples of the Toltec lineage.

With *Toltecs of the New Millennium*, Victor Sanchez offers

us the second part of his trilogy, in which he narrates his experience among the Toltec "survivors". In a personal style and
from an anti-anthropological perspective, he opens the door to
that parallel universe wherein dwell the Wirrarika, thus sup-
plying a living testimony about indigenous knowledge as
seen manifested from the inside.

Victor Sanchez is currently working on the third book of
the trilogy, in which the reader will encounter the key elements of a process of self-realization using the powerful tools
present in the Toltec Tradition which, he affirms, contains the
fundamental elements that can return dignity and magic to
our life experience which belong to us as luminous mortal
beings.

Meanwhile, Victor Sanchez continues his experiences
among the surviving Toltecs, not only to further his own
process of growth and investigation, but also to accomplish
the commitment made with the elders and the marakames of
the Sierra Wirrarika on November 15, 1993: to submit a written testimony about the Wirrarika Spiritual Tradition, not
directed toward the general public but to these same indigenous communities, thus breaking the existing tradition among
anthropologists and writers who generally do not return the
fruits of their labors to the communities in which their investigations are carried out. The aim is to contribute to the preservation of the traditions and practices partially described in
Toltecs of the New Millennium, now that the processes of alpha-
betization implemented in margined areas by the Mexican
Government are beginning to produce a relatively new phenomenon: Indians who can read books. The objective in gathering a written testimony about the Tradition is that the new
generations of Wirrarika, who are progressively learning how
to read, can read not only books having to do with the world
of the Tewaris (non-indigenous peoples), but also those which
speak of their own Tradition.

Aside from his experiences in the indigenous world,
Victor Sanchez spends a large part of his time giving

conferences, workshops, and seminars around the world, in which he is working to create a bridge that allows people living in large cities to nourish themselves with the magic that is preserved among indigenous communities of Toltec descent and which, without our being aware of it, hides one of the most priceless treasures ever generated by human experience on this Earth: the knowledge of the otherness.

Those wishing to contact the author by letter should write to:

Victor Sanchez
A.P. 12-762
C.P. 033001
Mexico, D.F. MEXICO